IMAGES
of Wales

MACHEN
REVISITED

GW00469501

Mynydd Machen, at the top of the photograph, has yielded evidence of prehistoric remains, namely pillow mounds (burial sites) in the area of Penrhiw Warren near the Ridgeway nature footpath, and close by are sites on which homesteads would have been situated. Flint awls used as scrapers, ascribed to the Neolithic age, *c.* 3500-1900 BC, and a palstave, which was a type of axe used before a socketed axe, *c.* 1400 to 1200 BC, have also been found in the same area. The pillow mounds and homesteads, thought to be of Bronze age origin, *c.* 1900-500 BC, can be seen at the top of the photograph. (Crown Copyright 1962/MOD)

Contents

Foreword

This book endeavours to trace the development of Machen, from its earliest days to the present time. It is not intended to be a definitive history, although a great deal of background source material has been included, to enrich a story of the Machen that many of us remember and love. The impressive collection of photographs made available to us, together with the reminiscences of so many people, have made it possible to visit once again, a different time and a different world.

None of this would have been achieved were it not for the actions of our late chairman, Eric Coleman. He, along with Delphine, other concerned locals such as Lloyd Davies, Arthur Rogers and others, started it all in 1995.

Dennis Spargo
August 2001

Eric John Coleman, 1921-1998.

Dedication

We dedicate this book to all those who have contributed in so many different ways to making Machen Remembered the success it has been, and particularly to those who are no longer with us.

The road out of Draethen towards Rudry in the early twentieth century.

One

In the Beginning

Machen's story cannot be understood fully without reference to local geology: its history is preserved in the rocks which surround it. A study of this, conducted over a great many years, has provided us with a layman's description which is understandable, fascinating and informative. Around 350 million years ago, the area of the village was under a sea whose bed was covered by a limey mud which gave Machen its quarry. When the limestone, known as dolomite, was folded and uplifted by earth movements, it was fractured and penetrated by super-heated gases which cooled to form minerals such as barytes, calcite, and most importantly, galena (lead ore).

This uplift of land placed Machen right on the shoreline; the locally named 'Devil broke his apron strings' is an old beach where rounded pebbles can be seen, while the name 'Traeth', given to the straight road leading from Lower Machen to Draethen, is Welsh for 'beach' or 'shore'. This area of Devon conglomerate (pudding stone) also shows sea-worn pebbles.

Machen became low-lying land just above sea level, and on its warm silts and brackish lagoons grew dense forests of giant ferns. As the sea level rose and fell, these were overwhelmed and re-established many times. Each forest was marked by a coal seam, which could vary locally in thickness from under an inch to over twenty feet. This represented thousands of years of uninterrupted plant growth. Fossil plants can still be found from these ancient 'everglades' in the tips left which we see today, left as a consequence of mining the coal.

An impressive example of these plants can be found in the Llanarth Street area of Chatham, Machen. The trunk of a giant fern, measuring fifty-five centimetres in width and one hundred centimetres in height, was unearthed when the coal seam at the top of the street was mined in the nineteenth century. It now has a preservation order on it.

Machen's oldest tree is more than 300 million years old. Several types of fern trunks can be seen in the National Museum in Cardiff, but our particular specimen is *Calamites Undulatus*, an old relative of the horsetail fern. *Calamites* were in the lower coal measures of the carboniferous period.

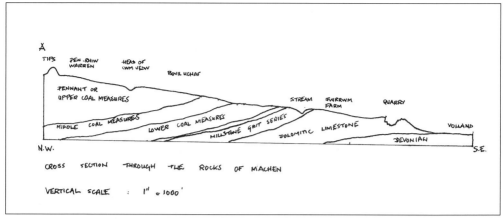

A cross section of the rocks at Machen.

Three hundred million years ago, Machen was in a shallow but slowly sinking sea, into which sand was deposited from nearby land masses. This resulted in the formation of pennant sandstone, hundreds of feet thick. Its thin beds yielded ideal stones for local walling, and much came from the two old quarries in the Cwm, while clay beds under the coal seams led to the setting up of the local brick-works.

The last million years have seen ten ice ages and intervening warmer periods. The last glacier came down the Rhymney Valley about 10,000 years ago, stopping at Bedwas where the comprehensive school is built on its terminal moraine, while Machen was partly covered by a marginal lake. The last 10,000 years have seen ice, frost, rain, streams and rivers wearing all the rocks mentioned into a fertile soil on the valley floor, which gave rise to dairy farming in the lower areas, and sheep farming on the hard rock of barren Mynydd Machen.

The Legacy of the Romans: Lead Mining

The mineral wealth of Great Britain was known to the Romans: Tacitus, one of their greatest historians and writers, stated it was one of the chief reasons for their invasions. The local geology possibly brought them to Machen, where they were working the lead mines at Cefn Pwll-du, certainly by AD 75 when their campaign in South Wales was completed. Lead continued to be mined in Machen during the time of Queen Elizabeth I, while an inventory in the Tredegar estate archives, lists the iron and tin pipes in 'the smith's forge by the upper level' of Machen lead mine in 1784. A lead ingot was found in the 1930s by Eric Coleman in the vicinity of Castell Meredydd.

Pottery

Pre-1909, several Roman coins had been found in the lead mine and, in 1921, excavations for sewers E.N.E. of Draethen bridge, yielded fragments of Samian-ware and coarse-ware pottery, together with a coin, all dating to the first and second centuries AD.

Further artefacts were discovered in 1937 when the workmen cut through occupation layers extending from the old Lower Machen post office, opposite the gates of Machen house, for a distance of some 400 yards east along the south edge of the old road. Lumps of lead ore were discovered, along with other finds which included fragments of quern stones for grinding ore, a complete floor tile, flagons, pots, bowls and so on.

Preparatory work for the new by-pass road at Lower Machen in 1937. Group with Ivor Norris and Jack Newton.

An example of Roman pottery found at Lower Machen, adjacent to St Michael's Church, during building work in 1996.

The Norman Influence

The location of Castell Meredydd, of which there is little to be seen today, was certainly a commanding one. Prior to the Norman Conquest, Wales consisted of several independent kingdoms, Machen being part of the area known as Gwynllwg. The many internal disputes between them made it easier for the invasions of the Normans who, in 1091 after many years of border parrying, finally overran and occupied the South Wales lowlands. The valleys and remoter areas of the hinterland remained in Welsh hands, with the holders acknowledging the 'over-lordship' of their conquerors.

Roads and Bridges

The roads and bridges of Machen are so much a part of our everyday existence that they are very much taken for granted. In medieval times, their maintenance was passed by the Lord of the Manor to the parish, and a surveyor was appointed to detail work required. Every able-bodied man had to give six days' unpaid labour a year, but if he could provide a cart and horses for hauling, he was excused paying his rates!

Machen highways accounts record excellent details of what was done in the eighteenth and nineteenth centuries. Stone for road repairs was hauled from the small quarries at Coed Cefn above Rhyd-y-Gwern; Caetirbach alongside the Run; Twyn Berllan, the forerunner of today's Machen quarry; Ocherwyth; Craig-yr-Rhacca; and the Gelli. Carts pulled by oxen and later by horses were used, together with sledges, the ends of which had to be steeled on occasion by the local blacksmith.

Representational drawing of Castle Meredydd, which stood on a rocky ledge above Machen quarry. It was built by Meredydd Gethin (the grandson of Rhys Tewdwr, a prominent Welshman who was slain in 1093), probably before 1115, when Gwynllwg was conquered. In 1263 the Norman family of de Clare captured the castle, and, although described as being habitable in 1314, nothing more appears to be known of its history.

The name lives on as the Machen Junior School has a house points system, and Meredydd is one of four houses, the others being Pandy, Chatham and Ruperra. Meredith House, winners on Sports day 1968.

Draethen bridge was known long ago as Machen bridge, and it necessitated many calls upon the parish purse. Up until 1753, it was built of wood, and on 5 June that year, Samuel Richard and Thomas Edmond of Trevethin, Masons, together with Joshua Watkins, Yeoman of Aberystruth (the old name for the Blaina district) executed a bond with the surveyors of Machen to build a stone bridge for the sum of £126.

The re-building merited many entries in parish records. These tell of compensation paid to two farmers for trespass, and damage done to their ground by the hauling of stones to the site. Roots had to be taken out from the old bridge, and labour found for making 'good and sufficient weirs'. Payment was also made for gathering and planting quicks (hawthorns) together with stakes and 'watlings' to set hedges nearby.

The bridge at Draethen originally had stone parapets in addition to its safety bays, but these were replaced with iron rails some years ago.

The stone bridge, also known as Pont-y-Draethen in the eighteenth century.

The Iron bridge is dated 1829. At this time, young Augustus Morgan, third son of Sir Charles Morgan of Tredegar House, was serving as curate at Lower Machen, becoming rector in 1831.

Near the old village was the Iron bridge (adjacent to Machen Plas farm) which was used by members of the Morgan family to attend church at Lower Machen, when in residence at Ruperra Castle. Close by is an attractive cottage, which was inhabited by an estate worker, usually one of the keepers, who looked after its maintenance. The track from Ruperra through the woods, across the bridge, and over the fields to the church must have been a delightful journey for the family and any guests, no doubt being transported in a coach and four. At Christmas time, there would be many important visitors at Ruperra, and the whole retinue would 'sweep' along the bridge and field watched by local children, who would find their interest rewarded by the throwing of coins from the carriages. Today, it is an area that abounds in wild garlic.

Turnpikes and Tolls

This was the era of toll roads and toll houses, when an effort was being made to improve conditions for travellers. In the late eighteenth century and early nineteenth century, the old highways records tell of the efforts made to keep the turnpike road in repair.

Paid £1 11s 6d for hedging and ditching by the new road.
Halling 66 loads of stone for turnpike road.
Throwing snow from the road 2 days.
William Rowland making and covering gutter in the turnpike road near Gelli.
Thomas John Howell with cart and 3 horses halling to repair road in bottom of Vorlan (Volland).
23 days cleaning watercourse, turnpike and by roads. £1 18s 4d.
Raising 225 perches of hazards on Machen turnpike road £2 6s 10d.
(A perch is a solid measure for stone, 16ft 6in x 18in x 12in.)

Church Records and the Old Poor Law

Civil registration commenced in 1837, but the church registers of births, marriages and burials begin in 1686. These contain information that reveals glimpses of those who made up the population of Machen in the seventeenth and eighteenth centuries. One learns of Edward Jaines, the hammer man; Philips Elis, carpenter; Edward Samuel, miner; John Lewis, collier (charcoal burner); John William, weaver; John Isaac, miller; Thomas Lewis, sawyer; Joseph Hussy, copperman; Thomas Harry, a brick man; and Harry Morgan, the tiler, all part of the village's industrial past.

The care of the poor was also part of the duties of the churchwardens and the overseers or guardians of the poor, although this duty was taken from them with the building of union workhouses from 1834 onwards. Very often these offices were combined, and a church rate and poor rate was levied on parishioners. Those who were in need were 'relieved' by way of weekly payments, and having house rents paid. Provision was made for purchase of new boots, and repairs included soling and capping. Flannel from the Pandy mill was purchased for shirt making and cloth for making breeches, together with coats, aprons, caps and stockings. Malt and barley, bacon, sugar, bread, oatmeal, mutton, cheese and butter, together with bedding and sacks of coals were regularly dispensed, and a surgeon was retained and paid to attend 'the paupers'. Often the full expenses of a funeral were accounted for out of the poor rate. This would include the coffin, shroud, soap, candles, tea, sugar and cheese.

Money was left by Hugh Jones of Gelliwastaad, in 1777, and Madam Katharina Morgan of Ruperra in 1720, in order that land should be purchased and the rent used to buy bread and blankets for those in need, as well as providing 'twenty shillings per annum to pay for ye schooling of two poor boys of the parish forever'.

Lower Machen still has its old toll house, which was carefully sited to gather tolls from travellers on the Draethen and Rhyd-y-gwern lanes, those passing along the old road from Newport to Caerphilly via the Volland, and those travelling over the mountain to Risca.

Other Parish Expenditure

Other duties of the parish officers included paying out the odd few coppers, which probably made the difference between starving and existing, to those who killed vermin and brought them as proof of so doing. Hedgehogs, wild cats, badgers, foxes and pine martins would merit from 4d to 6d each. Very often the money was paid to widows. One item records 'ketching oonts in the churchyard and killing an adder', 'oont' being an old word for a mole. Wool was given for weaving and tools provided to enable the poor to make a living.

The maintenance of the church itself in those days included whitening the walls, 10s; buying new bell ropes, 6s; mending the bible, 4s, and so on. Larger repair works must have been difficult, since ladders had to be fetched from Ruperra at a cost of 1s 6d for a man and horse. Tiling the roof in 1745 involved carriage of 1500 tile stones, 500 lathes, ale for the tiler; together with hair, nails and lime, lath nails and poles for scaffolding. Likewise when the churchyard wall was repaired at the same time, a team of six oxen was employed for two days to haul sand and stone. When a new ceiling was installed in 1808, the entry merits inclusion for its information, spelling and dialect!

'Building to make the roof and ceiling. New ceiling put in. Making a cornish £6. Ally blaster for the cornish. New pews, floor and gallery posts. Drawing the old roof down. Stripping the old tile of the church. Rising the copples'.

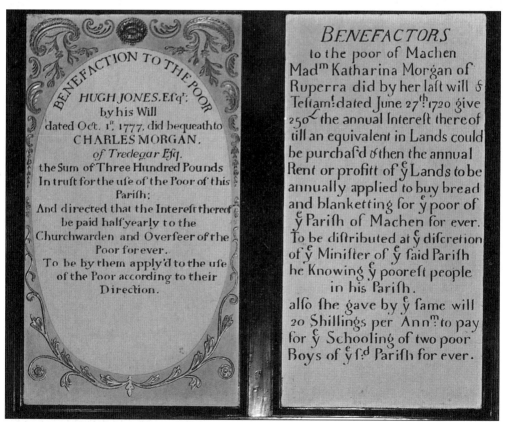

Charity board in St Michael's. The capital, which yields very little interest, has now been passed, with Charity Commission approval, to the Machen Rotary Club to be used for their charitable work in the area at Christmas.

The Tramroad and 'The Run'

Around 1826 the industrial pace of Machen quickened, when William and Joseph Russell took over Machen forge, enlarging and adapting it to manufacture tinplate. This coincided with the passing of an act in 1825 to build the Rumney tramroad to enable coal and iron to be transported direct from Rhymney to Newport docks quicker and more cheaply. The Old Rumney, as it later came to be known, started at Pye Corner in 1826, and was running through Machen around 1828. Its construction led to the opening up of more industry in the area including the Machen foundry and the Bovil coal level which encouraged the influx of workers with their families from many areas of the country.

Above: The impressive tomb of Joseph Russell of Gelliwastadd in the churchyard at Lower Machen. He died in 1865.

Right: The Run. All that remain today are a few stones with holes to show where the old rails were bolted, some showing rare iron fittings.

The Run, with the only remaining cottage of six, which housed workers from the Tin works. Another was used for a time as National Works School. The area was, and still is, known as Cae Bach.

The tramroad was connected to Machen forge, and later to the old pit adjacent to Green Row, by a railed way known then and now as 'The Run'. The Run would have been a busy place with trams and horses toiling to and fro from dawn to dusk taking their loads up to the tramroad, which later became the fondly-remembered Brecon and Merthyr railway.

One description of the activities came from Rector Augustus Morgan. He obviously had great influence over the parish, and was very much against the whole undertaking, particularly the changes which industry had wrought on rural areas. 'In my opinion, a tramroad for the conveyance of coal from the hills, to the sea-port for exportation, tends to demoralise the district through which it passes to an inconceivable degree. The results are theft, drunkenness and prostitution.'

Tramroad Pubs

The building of the tramroad led to the appearance of public houses, which were sited close to it in order to provide refreshment for the hauliers and their animals. The Rising Sun, The White Hart and the 'old' Royal Oak were all sited very close to the tramroad, and were built in the 1830s.

The Rising Sun was part of the Tredegar estate until its sale in 1920, and has been a private dwelling for many years, although the worn incised lettering of its origins can still be seen on the stone gatepost.

I have very happy memories of the Rising Sun. In the early 1940s, I was a student teacher evacuated to Trethomas with a class of children from Gillingham. Most of my colleagues were elderly having returned to take over from those in the forces, and nearly every weekend we would walk there. It was always well-patronised; the lovely views and hospitality remain in my memory. (B. Shilleto)

The White Hart was the next focal point on the tramroad, also owned by the Tredegar estate. It was tenanted by several members of the Vaughan family from the early nineteenth century, one of whom was manager of the tramroad. At one time there was a pond in the field behind the building, where the horses were watered while the hauliers had their refreshment. This was later filled in when the railway came into being. The building now contains some fine wood panelling, purchased when a large liner was broken up in Newport many years ago.

16

The White Hart which, for many years, was run by the Kellow family followed by Charles and 'Nanna' Gadd.

The 'old' Royal Oak was not only very close to the tramroad, but also to the old trackway over the mountain to Risca.

Rural Machen, prior to the accession of Queen Victoria, was poised to build upon its early industrial background, which existed owing to its mineral resources and their proximity to each other. It also possessed, thanks to the efforts of Revd Augustus Morgan, a school in Lower Machen, which he established in 1834, several decades before education became compulsory.

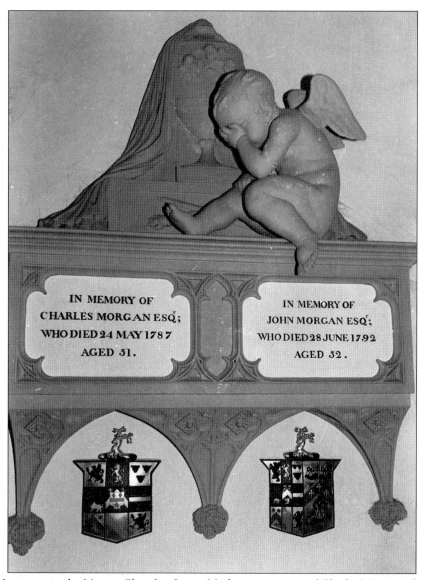

IN MEMORY OF
CHARLES MORGAN ESQ;
WHO DIED 24 MAY 1787
AGED 51.

IN MEMORY OF
JOHN MORGAN ESQ;
WHO DIED 28 JUNE 1792
AGED 52.

Wall Monument in the Morgan Chapel at Lower Machen, in memory of Charles Morgan, who died in 1787 aged fifty-one, and his brother John Morgan, who died in 1792 aged fifty-two. They were the last male heirs of the Morgan line, the estate devolving on their sister Jane, who had married in 1758, Charles Gould, later to become Judge Advocate General, Sir Charles Gould.

Sir Charles Gould was granted the name of Morgan by Royal Licence. He was a man of great ability and interests. He promoted local canal building, leased much of the estate for iron working and coal mining, and encouraged the building of The Sirhowy to Newport tramroad. One mile of the tramroad passed through Tredegar Park, which became known as the 'golden mile' because of the toll paid to the estate for every truck passing over it. Sir Charles Gould died in 1806.

Two
How the Village Expanded

In 1839, two years after the accession of the young Queen Victoria to the throne, the Chartist Riots erupted, led by John Frost, William Jones and Zephaniah Williams. Zephaniah Williams, soon after his marriage, lived in Machen at Bovil house, which had been built by his father-in-law. His brother-in-law, Dr John Llewellyn of The Twyn, Caerphilly, later married into the Woodruff family, and had a Machen surgery in Doctor's Row. John Llewellyn made arrangements for Zephaniah's escape to Australia, but Zephaniah was captured and transported to Tasmania where he remained for the rest of his life. After being granted a free pardon, he became a successful coal owner.

Two events which were to prove of vital importance occurred early in Queen Victoria's reign. One was the publication of tithe maps, and the other was the commencement of detailed official census records in 1841.

The tithe map and its accompanying details show that there was a village pound in Lower Machen, adjacent to the old school. This was a small enclosure, usually walled or fenced in the centre of a village, where wandering cows and sheep were impounded, and only released on

Property built on the site of the 'Parish Houses' in Lower Machen by the Tredegar Estate, after their demolition, c. 1854.

payment of a fine. These were erected by order of ancient Manorial Courts and maintained by them.

Close by the pound and the old school were some 'parish houses' as they were called, which were parish property administered by the Poor Law guardians. Poor Law accounts regularly mention repairs to windows, floor and fireplaces, and in one instance, the making of a new oven, requiring twelve days work on the part of the mason and his labourer, eight sacks of lime, carriage of sand and eighteen horse-loads of stones.

The new Poor Law Act of 1834 directed that all parish poor houses should be sold, and indoor parish relief only given in the newly built union workhouses. The 1851 Machen Census shows that the parish houses were in a state of disrepair, and were occupied by four elderly folk classed as 'paupers'.

Machen's tithe map is dated 1842, and shows every road, railway, path, meadow, wood, and building that existed at that date. These maps were prepared for the whole country by qualified surveyors, and gave acreage and the amount due from occupiers to those who were entitled to the tithe. In the medieval period, this consisted of a tenth of certain grains and produce, which was given to the rector or tithe holder of a parish as part of income. However, in 1842 this was commuted to a cash payment. The map records the exisence of Bovil Colliery, the foundry, Machen forge, quarries, lime kilns, Machen Corn Mill and the Pandy tucking mill, together with Weavers Row newly-built for its workers.

No buildings existed on the south side of the road between the Fwrwm Ishta and the Yard, today known as Bronrhiw, but in 1842 known as Fwrrwm Ucha homestead.

The triangle on which the infants' school was to be built is shown as a garden belonging to the forge. Today it is the church hall.

The top side of the road was partially developed, with a blacksmith's shop opposite the school site. Siloam chapel, and a few cottages are shown before reaching the two cottages at the bottom of the Dranllwyn lane.

The Run connected with the Rumney tramroad, which ran up the road and crossed near the Wesleyan chapel, consisting of two dwellings, continuing through the hamlet of White Hart which contained many dwellings occupied by forge workers.

Cottage at White Hart belonging to the Hicks family, several generations of which worked in the old Forge and Tin Works. The stones surmounting the wall are solid clinker from the forge workings.

The parish had many farms, the names of which remain today, although the homesteads have now become dwelling houses, with much of the land added to larger farms. In 1842 the acreage varied from smallholdings of twenty to thirty acres, to the majority which were seventy to eighty acres, and up to those with a hundred acres and more. Fwrrwm farm had 130 acres, and the largest holding was Machen Plas with 289 acres. On the smallholdings, family members were normally sufficient to cope with the husbandry skills required; only the large farms employed agricultural labourers and farm servants.

The easier transport to the docks afforded by the tramroad led to the need not only for the building of public houses, but of housing for those who immigrated to Machen as its industrial base expanded.

The recently introduced tinplating at the Forge was flourishing by the 1840s, and the Brass Foundry and the Bovil Colliery were also well established. The old pit, adjacent to Green Row – which had been worked for Revd Augustus Morgan on a small scale in the mid-1830s, mainly for estate purposes with a limited supply for neighbouring tenants, and then abandoned – was re-opened in 1850.

Right: The Rogers family at Ysgubor Fach.

Rose Cottages at the top of Church Street, once called Fwrrwm Lane. Close by was a forge and nailer's shop, overlooked by the Foundry.

21

A remarkable photograph showing New Row, Woodbine Terrace (the four houses), Twyn Sych, the ruins of the Coed Cefn Fire Brick Works and Colliers Row in the foreground.

Chatham Street with milk cart, cobbled drainage channels and rutted road surface. Housing here and in Llanarth Street provided homes for those working in the Bovil Colliery.

Colliers Row, known today as Riverside Terrace and originally known as River Row, was built around 1850 and was mainly occupied by those working at the old pit, which could be reached by using a bridge over the river between the houses. This was swept away by a storm during the First World War. The barracks in Green Row were also built at this time. Although divided into four houses for over a century, the buildings were originally inter-connected by a passage, which ran from end to end. It was a type of 'barracks' used by local workmen. New Row, variously named Mount Pleasant and Long Row, was built in 1854. The twenty dwellings often housed two families each, many of whom worked in the forge and tin works.

Alma Street, Lewis Street, Pandy Row, part of Wyndham Street, and Station Terrace were all built in the 1850s and 60s, but it was not until the 1891 census that many street names began to appear.

Tredegar Arms. One-time headquarters of a boxing club, where well-known local boxer Jack Newton did his training in the '20s. The landlord at this time was Thomas Rosser.

The 'new' Royal Oak opened in 1892, and became the venue for members of the Lodge of the Independent Order of Odd Fellows, who originally met at the 'old' Oak. At a later date, the quarry offices were housed there.

The rest of Machen's public houses were built, and became integrated into these new areas of population. The Lamb (known today as the Forge Hammer), the Roller's (now the Tradesman's Arms), and The Crown in Llanarth Street, are all recorded in the early 1850s, together with the Lewis's Hotel and the Tredegar Arms built a few years later. The Crown and Tredegar Arms are now private houses.

Upper Machen was rapidly becoming a village in its own right, and the need to provide a nearer place of worship brought about the building of St John's church in 1855. Originally known as a 'chapel of ease', it was not licensed for marriages until 1899.

Alongside the church came the non-conformist chapels, the earliest being the original Siloam, which was built in 1837, the year of the Queen's accession. Fuller descriptions of the chapels can be found in *Machen Remembered*, published by Tempus in 1996.

The rector, Augustus Morgan, realising the big changes taking place in the village, actually made three censuses himself, in 1839, 1844 and 1853, in addition to the official records made every decade. Fortunately for Machen, he knew the value of education, and built three schools in addition to the one in Lower Machen, on land given by his father.

In addition to his 1853 Census, he listed the name and age of every child attending school, together with the occupation and residence of their parents. Interesting facts emerge from these school attendance lists: for instance, there were 92 infants from Upper Machen in the church room school; while Lower Machen school, which catered mainly for older children, had 79 pupils; and Waun Fawr school, which was located in the parish on the Risca side of the mountain with most pupils on the Machen side of the valley, had 79 pupils. All the children paid school pence.

The old school over the river (at Glan-yr-Afon) was not built until 1873, so older scholars from Upper Machen made the journey to Lower Machen.

Of the 79 pupils at Waun Fawr, 57 had fathers who were colliers. Fathers of pupils at Upper and Lower Machen schools were hammerers, rollers, doublers, picklers, tinmen, finers, bar rollers and so on, all working in the forge, together with engineers, masons, farmers, quarrymen, publicans, carpenters, blacksmiths, grocers, a tailor, sawyers, weavers, brickmakers, millers and labourers. The number of children in the village in 1853 was 1,072, 675 of whom were under the age of 12, so some 25% were receiving education, which was a creditable achievement.

The Rumney tramroad, which had earlier stimulated the growth of Upper Machen, was proving to be quite dangerous with its combination of flange and edge-rails and the congestion of trams, carts and pedestrians using it. By 1854 the addition of steam engines restricted to a 10mph speed limit made modernisation necessary.

Machen in the late nineteenth century. Forge Road was a narrow lane with tall hedges, loaded with honey-suckle and dog roses.

Original tramroad mile sign, photographed in situ at Machen Fach in the 1950s by S.C. Phillips, a well-known railway photographer. It is now in the local museum at Risca.

Interior of the B & M Workshop, c. 1900. The 'gaffer' with the bowler hat is Herbert Jones, Deputy Superintendent of the Brecon & Merthyr Railway, and manager of the workshops in Machen.

The tramroad became the Rumney Railway Company in 1861, but it was not until the Brecon and Merthyr Railway Company took over in 1863 that the necessary changes took place. This led to the development in 1868-1870 of the B & M engine works and carriage repair depot near to the Machen foundry.

The area of Machen sheds must have been a very busy and noisy place by the 1870s. The main railway line traversed it, and it was near to the Machen foundry run by Philip Woodruff who now owned the Machen iron and tin works. The foundry built wagons, and manufactured all types of railway plant. There was also a weighbridge close to Bovil house.

25

The proximity of the Woodruff residence, the Vedw, to the station and the workshops was often a cause of friction. Philip Woodruff writing in his diary complains of 'engines whistling from 4.30 to 6.30 in the morning, and late at night when I am smoking a pipe'. There were also problems with water which was needed for the foundry and very often was not available because the 'Railway Company had the whole of the brook turned to their reservoir by the station'.

The business of John Brewer, who originally came to Machen around 1848, as agent for the Rumney Tramroad, and later manager of the Rumney Railway, was also adjacent to the workshops. He lived, first of all, in Birchwood Cottage, later known as the Vedw, and eventually tenanted Bovil farm. Together, with his son Samuel, he worked the Bovil Colliery, and the Sun Level nearby. They also ran a saw mill, in addition to manufacturing firebricks,

Interior of Machen shops (in later years), showing belt driven machinery. (NMGW, Department of Industry)

The modern development of Crown Walk is built around the area of the Bovil Colliery, and mention is made of John Brewer's coal and clay levels in some of the Deeds.

Chatham Place, built in 1850, was known many years ago as Chatham Row and Rainers Row. James Rainer was a groom and native of Kent, who lived in Draethen.

railway fencing, and many types of railway equipment. He had a large family of twelve children, one of whom, a boy of eleven, was drowned in the river near the weir at Machen. The weddings of several of his children were village events with firing of cannon most of the day, and his workmen being treated to a meal at Lewis's Hotel. He and his wife ended their days in Machen in 1886 and 1888 respectively, and are buried in St John's churchyard.

The parish was now able to offer employment, housing, education, places of worship, and with the establishment of the Friendly Society Movement in the early nineteenth century, there was the opportunity to contribute for a 'rainy day' when there might be loss of wages due to illness, or death. It was also insurance against the dreaded union workhouses. Old records show that a branch of the Independent Order of Odd Fellows was functioning in Machen by 1843, meeting at the old Royal Oak. Members could buy regalia consisting of emblems, scarves, and rosettes with oak leaves. Account books for the period 1865-1871 show payments ranging from 3s 4d to £1 6s 8d, while generous donations were made for funerals, from £12 to £16. Membership at that time was 160.

The Royal Oak Lodge of the Oddfellows Order, owned the leases of Chatham Row, and had money invested in the English Wesleyan chapel. From the newspaper report following it would appear that there were two branches of the Order of Oddfellows in the village, one in Upper Machen and one in Draethen, possibly inaugurated by Mr Rainer since it was named Medway. The Draethen lodge also owned leases of houses known as Draethen Club Row in the Chatham area.

Monmouthshire Merlin 25 June 1852

On Monday the 14th inst., the anniversary of the Medway Lodge of the Independent Order of Oddfellows, meeting at the Holly Bush, Draythan was held. About ten o'clock between fifty and sixty of the members met at their club house, and having formed themselves into procession, headed by the Machen band, marched to its enlivening music to the Machen church, where the Revd Augustus Morgan, MA, preached a very interesting and appropriate sermon.

After divine service the brethren walked as far as brother David Jones's Rollers Arms, (Tradesmens Arms), the band bringing together the inhabitants in large numbers, who pronounced the procession to be the best turn out hitherto seen in Machen. After refreshing themselves a little, they returned to the lodge room, where host Jones had provided an excellent dinner, to which the members, with several visitors, did ample justice. The chairman for the event was John Llewellyn, surgeon of the lodge.'

Dr Llewellyn was also the practitioner employed by Machen Foundry which had a Works fund to which employees contributed to enable them to receive benefit and medical treatment. An old account book of 1874 records that 17 men paid varying amounts of 6d, 1s and 2s per month. He received the contributions and charged 3s 6d in addition for one joint examination.

The Revd Augustus Morgan founded the reading room, which in 1864 was described as being 'well supplied with daily and weekly newspapers, periodicals, etc., supported by subscriptions'. By 1893 this was open twelve hours a day, members paying 5s a year, and working men 1d a week. There was also a small library attached, open for an hour a week. This is better known today as Machen Rugby Club.

Mr Edwards (owner of the old post office), supplied the local reading rooms with all papers, of which we had a good supply daily, and once a month the Science Siftings and Quiver were delivered. The Parish Council paid up regularly, also paying the delivery fee of 19s 6d per quarter, which Mr Edwards kept for himself, although it was we girls who took the papers down, or someone who was passing. (Mrs A. Edmunds)

Machen's sporting heritage commenced in 1871 with the founding of the rugby club, followed by the cricket club in 1878. The following extract from *The Welsh Athlete* of 5 October 1891 gives some idea of the obstacles that had to be overcome.

Machen Greys Football and Athletic Club

For several years the club has struggled along against difficulties that would have daunted any less determined young fellows, their greatest difficulty being a suitable field for play. Mr F. Stratton has permitted games to be played in his fields at Lower Machen, free of cost, but as they were nearly two miles away from Machen Upper, there was always difficulty in getting members to practice, consequently cricket has not made the progress it would have under more favourable circumstances.

Football was played in a field at Machen Upper, kindly placed at their disposal by Mrs Thomas of the Fwrrwm Ishta Inn, but as the game had to be played up or down a hill, visiting teams did not care about playing at Machen. Now through the good offices of the Revd J.C.S. Darby, the committee have secured a field suitable for cricket, lawn tennis and football, and there is not a more suitable field within 20 miles of Machen. (The field was situated near the viaduct and tin works).

One of the best performers in the Machen Greys was Harry Harris. He was one of the first rugby players to 'go north'. Sometime in 1896/7, Harry Harris and another of the Grey's men called Mayberry, went up to Salford to play in a trial game. At the end of the game the officials of the club called Harry in to interview him. They offered him a contract and a house to live in, with immediate effect. Harry said 'what about my butty Mayberry?' and they told him they couldn't find a place for Mayberry. Harry thought it over for a while, and then said 'if you can't find a place for my butty, then I shan't accept your offer'. Then he went to the station and went home again, incidentally, leaving Mayberry behind in a pub! (Russell Harris)

Machen Greys Rugby Team in the late nineteenth century. From left to right, back row: H.G. Jones, E. Davis. Second row: A. Skuse, C. Underwood, E. Rodway, J. Potter, G. Neal, W. Thomas, W.E. Davis. Third row: A. Leonard, G. Phillips, J. Richton (Capt), W. Willans, S. Mayberry, A. Jenkins. Front row: A. Llewellyn, H. Harris, H. Prosser, M. Davis, J. Davis.

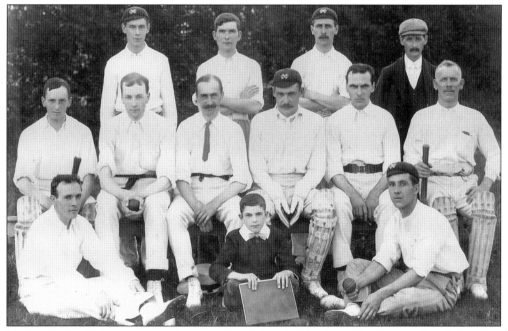

Machen Cricket Club, early twentieth century. From left to right, back row: Bert Beeston, Penry Lewis, John Arthur Thomas, Dai Mayberry. Middle row: Roland Stratton, Arthur Stratton, Leolin Forestier Walker, Charles Underwood (Pro), -?-, Bill Harris. Front row: Tom Williams, Tal Buckley, Sid Smith.

Machen Rectory, today a private dwelling. In Victorian times, it had extensive grounds, part of which were sold for housing known as Rectory Gardens. A smaller modern rectory was built nearby.

Girls exercising with dumb-bells in the old school playground at Glan-yr-Afon.

Schools

The 1870s saw changes in parish life. Upper Machen now had its own junior mixed school, opened in 1873 and situated on the Glamorgan side of the river at Glan-yr-Afon. It catered for boys and girls, and had both a headmaster and headmistress. Two years later in 1875, the Revd Augustus Morgan died; and the old rectory in Lower Machen, in which he had resided for over forty years, became a private house owned by the Tredegar Estate, a new rectory having been built in Upper Machen.

By the end of the century, the Upper Machen junior school at Glan-yr-Afon was in the charge of Mr G.D. Inkin, who took over after the untimely death of the previous headmaster, Mr E. Connor. The headmistress was a Mrs Jones from Merthyr Tydfil.

Mrs Jones lived at Chatham Villa, and her maid brought her a jug of tea and a plate of hot buttered toast, several rounds, every morning about 10 o'clock, which she cleared as soon as the registers were called. Our new schoolmaster was Mr G.D. Inkin. He was a big improvement by way of looks and smartness, and in no time had a piano brought into the boys' school, which did not please the girls. To balance things, Mr Inkin gave a number of us a voice test, and we used to go to the boys' school for our singing lessons afterwards. We loved singing for Mr Inkin; he was very brilliant in those days. (Mrs A. Edmunds)

30

In 1893 the infants' school was enlarged as a result of inspectors' reports over the years. A new schoolroom and cloak-room for the infants was added; a few years prior a gallery had been installed. This was a slightly raised platform that enabled the teacher to see pupils better when there were so many in one room. The headmistress or 'governess' as she was known in those days, was Miss Annie Williams, who commenced in 1893 and remained until 1925. She was described by one of her pupils, Mrs Alice Edmunds, as 'tall and slim, with lovely long golden hair which she wore in a plait wound round her head, set off with two tortoiseshell hairpins, or a fancy comb'.

Machen Infants School, possibly prior to 1893 when the building was enlarged. From left to right: Miss E. Potter, Miss A. Williams, Miss B. Henney. So many children in one large room would be unpopular with today's regulations. Infections must have spread quickly.

Mr G.D. Inkin and pupils at the old Junior School, sometime between 1899 and 1907.

Mixed class with headmistress in the late 1890s.

Francis Thompson, the longest serving teacher at any of the schools. Appointed Headmaster of Lower Machen School in 1834, he was still teaching there in 1873, dying in Lower Machen in 1899, at the age of 93. He also served as Clerk to the Parish Council for many years. The school closed towards the end of the nineteenth century.

As the close of the century approached, Machen forge and tin works, which had been working to capacity with 232 employees, was experiencing financial difficulties. In 1884 it had merged with the Waterloo tin plate works which opened in 1876. Philip Woodruff died in 1885, and although his sons carried on running the company, which included the Coed Cefn brickworks and Pentwyn pit, it did not prosper. The business was auctioned in 1886, and all the machinery, together with wagons, trams, tools and brick making plant, was sold without reserve. Also included were agricultural implements, carts, ploughs and animals including horses, sheep and cattle.

Although the old Machen forge was never worked again, the Waterloo tin works were operating by 1893, having been taken over by the owner of the Pontymister Tinplate Company. Two years later it was taken over by Richard Thomas, who was connected with the Melingriffith tin works.

Classroom in the 'old' school over the river, the only photograph of the interior so far traced. Late nineteenth century.

Samuel Winmill and his wife Elizabeth, who lived in one of the houses known as Winmill Terrace, later Woodbine Terrace. Samuel worked in Machen Tin Works. He died in 1893, two months after his wife.

Holidays for those at work were confined to the main festivals, Christmas, Good Friday etc. Children, however, had a three week summer holiday and were often given a half day's holiday if the school was required for other purposes, for example, a dinner for the choirs of both churches, harvest festival, Good Friday, the village Eisteddfod, and sometimes after the examination by HM Inspector. Fairs, picnics, tea parties given by the Band of Hope, circus visits, and club walks were all occasions for community involvement.

Y Gymanfa Ganu

'Machen people gathered together for a whole week while it was in progress, and wonderful singing was enjoyed in English and Welsh. The Gymanfa was held in a large field at the end of Wyndham Street. Italian minstrels used to visit Machen bringing their hurdy-gurdy and dear little love-birds in a cage on top. If we gave a penny, the little bird would hop on a stick carried by the minstrel, and take out a card from the little drawer to give to a child. Then there was the Armenian family who camped for a week somewhere in the woods and had a big brown bear which could dance. The man had tin clappers on his head, from which a leather strap was brought under his heel to which a ring of bells was fastened, and then he would give a long-drawn note on his concertina, and the bear would lift himself on to his hind legs and dance.

The Eisteddfod

The Fwrrwm Ishta field was ideal for the Eisteddfod, as lots of people could use the natural slope for seats. Mr Wm Ebrill Edwards, the postmaster and a composer, did extremely well for he sold hundreds of copies of his compositions, not to mention the hundreds of local view postcards and small china "Coat of Arms" of the Tredegar family, who were ever popular.' (Mrs A. Edmunds)'

The Fwrrwm Ishta is the oldest pub in Machen. Land tax records list it in 1752. It was used for many Tredegar Estate functions, and for Queen Victoria's Golden and Diamond Jubilee celebrations in 1887 and 1897, when dinner was served to everyone in the parish over fifty years of age, and tea was provided for all the children. The licensee during the 1890s was a widow and described thus:

Mrs Thomas managed the Fwrrwm Ishta. No one dared say a word out of place, she had the look of a real lady, always dressed in black, and a gold watch and chain round her neck. She had her nearly white hair dressed in the fashionable 'teapot handle' style and a very large tortoiseshell comb. When the 'Mari Llwyd' visited Machen at Christmas, she would send her nice maid, Miss Brangham, upstairs to watch for the procession. Whichever pub they called at always handed out refreshments, and Mrs Thomas would hand out drinks through a downstairs window. (Mrs A. Edmunds)

(The Mary Llwyd is an ancient Welsh custom at Christmas, still practised in a few places, in which a disguised group of men parade with the leader wearing a horse's head, exacting tributes of money, food, or drink from houses in the locality.)

The Church Supper

All the elderly church members were invited to supper, which was spread out in the rectory dining room. Evergreens were a favourite for decorations; the lovely tall brass candlesticks had a lighted candle in each one, and those rooms were very lovely indeed. No curtains were drawn those nights, and people used to gather on the rectory lawn to have a peep inside. John Arthue Potter, Edward Davey, Richard Trew and Tom Phillips sang the old favourites so all could join in the chorus. (Mrs A. Edmunds)

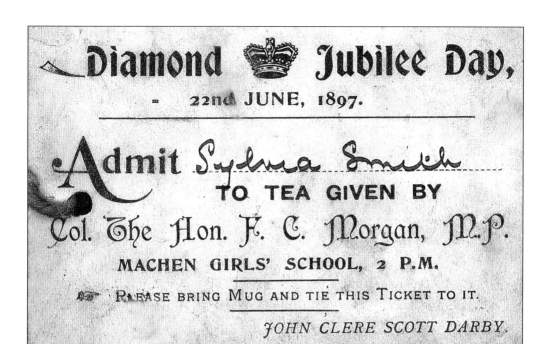

Diamond ✦ Jubilee Day,
22nd JUNE, 1897.

Admit *Sylvia Smith*
TO TEA GIVEN BY
Col. The Hon. F. C. Morgan, M.P.
MACHEN GIRLS' SCHOOL, 2 P.M.
PLEASE BRING MUG AND TIE THIS TICKET TO IT.
JOHN CLERE SCOTT DARBY.

Admission ticket for a Diamond Jubilee tea party in 1897. John Clere Scott Darby was Rector of Machen from 1873.

Sylvia Smith of Green Row ready to join in the celebration. The Golden Jubilee tea party for children, held in 1887, cost £9 3s 0d, which included 300 lbs of cake, 200 lbs of bread, 20lbs of butter, 50lbs of sugar and 5 gallons of milk.

The Boer War commenced two years after the Queen's Diamond Jubilee in 1897, and William Beechey, who worked on the Tredegar Estate, wrote in his diary '1899. Oct. We are having war with the Boers. Lord Tredegar sent 16 horses. Collected at the dinner of the grand meet for the widdows and wifes and children of the solders that is going out to Transvaal, a very good thing. £5.'

One little girl's memory was somewhat different! She wrote:
'During the Boer War we had a half day holiday for the relief of Ladysmith and Mafeking, when we composed our own little chorus to sing:

> "Lords Roberts and Kitchener, Generals Buller and White,
> They are very good generals, always ready for fight.
> And when we catch Kruger, how happy we'll be,
> We'll bring him back to old England, and give him a cold cup of tea.'"

The old industry of iron and tin working coupled with the closure of the Bovil Colliery levels in the early 1890s, signalled the decline of what had been the life blood of the community. However, the Waterloo tin works were still in operation, together with the much older working of the quarry.

The reign of Victoria spanned sixty-four years, which were momentous in the history of Machen. It commenced as an age of horse-power, and the old horse-troughs in Upper and Lower Machen are reminders of the need to cater for those attending church on horseback, as well as for those who toiled on up the mountain, in both areas. It ended with railway travel commonplace, Machen being in the forefront of the engineering required in this area to maintain it.

The Queen died at Osborne House, in the Isle of Wight, on 22 January 1901.

Machen Quarry, in the days of true horse power, at the end of the nineteenth century.

Above left: Victorian water trough in Church Street, Upper Machen.

Above right: Victorian water trough in Lower Machen.

Bottom left: Letter box at Lower Machen, bearing the letters VR. The universal penny post was introduced in 1840.

We were very sorry when HM Queen Victoria died, and did not play outdoor games that week, and all the daily papers had wide black lines though them and a picture of HM on the front page. (Mrs A. Edmunds)

Forge Cottages, Lower Machen, showing mounting steps. At one time, there was also a huge stone under one of the windows, on which bearers would rest coffins after a long walk on their way to the parish church.

Commerative mug for Queen Victoria's Diamond Jubilee 1937-1897.

Three
The Edwardian Age 1901-1910

The prospect of celebrations for the Coronation of Edward VII would have been a welcome holiday for many, and William Beechey recorded in his diary:

'1902. 14 May. They are making a bonfire on Machen mountain.
20 June. They have finished the bonfire on Machen mountain.'

Fate stepped in when the King was taken ill with appendicitis. Although the Coronation did not take place until 9 August, instead of 26 June, school tea parties were held as planned; bonfires and fireworks were finally set off on June 30.

I well remember the bonfire on Machen mountain, and much hard work was called for in order to haul wood, tar barrels and paraffin-soaked sacking up to the top, where a strong fence was erected around the space where the pile was to be built up. Alfred Rogers, Ysgubor Fach farm, had a team of mules who took all the heavy loads up the mountain. A strong platform held the pile, and on the night of the fire crowds of people assembled. Only two men were allowed inside the barrier, the man who fired the gun, and the man who lit the fire, which was done by means of a bundle of paraffin-soaked

The bonfire on Machen Mountain, marking the coronation of Edward VII: one of many lit across the country.

sacking tied to a very long pole. A match set this alight, and the man holding it would then set it on to the pile, which was soon sending flames leaping up. The bonfire was a great sight, but not greater than the silence kept while we waited to hear the gun sending out a signal. (Mrs A. Edmunds)

The new era also brought to a close the ministry in Machen of the Revd John Clere Scott Darby, who died in 1901. He came to the parish in 1873, taking over from the Revd Augustus Morgan, and was a greatly loved and respected man, 'being especially tender with aged and sick people'. He was a member of the school board and visited regularly with his first wife, who died in 1889. He had several sons by his first marriage, and re-married in 1892, his bride being Miss Emily Potter, a member of a well-known Machen family. Their only child, William Clere Augustus Darby, was killed in the First World War.

Everyone called him Bill, and he was a darling, for he loved having lots of children to play at the rectory, when we enjoyed tea on the lawns and swings on the oak trees. There were two beautifully kept lawns, The Shawl and The Croquet. (Mrs A. Edmunds)

In later years the Revd Darby suffered badly from rheumatism and gout. He was so keen on carrying out his duties that he would be wheeled in a barrow from the rectory to the church. They used to expect his best sermons when he suffered most! (Mrs M. Jones)

We shed tears at the passing of the Revd Darby, and we church children gathered lots of violets and primroses which we tied into little posies so that Mrs J.A. Potter could line the grave for him. We little choir girls wore a white blouse with a black velvet bow, but others wore black sateen blouses with white feather stitching on the cuffs and collars. (Mrs A. Edmunds)

New parish boundaries, established in 1894, meant that education in Machen was now carried out in the infant school in the church hall at the top of Forge Road, and the junior school for boys and girls by the river at Glan-yr-Afon. The school at Waun Fawr was now part of Risca parish.

Although the buildings of the junior school were censured for being cold and draughty, the desks in urgent need of replacement and the playground in a very bad condition, the standard of education had greatly improved. The minutes of the County Council Education Committee record that three of Mr Inkin's pupils had been awarded scholarships out of the seven available for the district. By 1904 Mr Inkin was teaching evening classes in Arithmetic, Maths and Drawing, with Shorthand, Machine Drawing, Geometry, and Applied Maths being taught by visiting tutors.

By 1905, the deterioration of the junior school buildings was causing much concern. A report was made to the Education Committee recommending that a new mixed and infants' school should speedily be erected, in order to accommodate 250 juniors and 200 infants, and a suitable site was to be negotiated with Lord Tredegar. The new school would be called Machen Council school.

Until the new building was completed, the Education Committee appointed a sub-committee in November 1906 to arrange temporary premises 'for children from Glamorgan school'. This was to take the form of a 'movable iron building to accommodate 300 children'.

I remember the tin school. It stood on the site almost immediately occupied by Meyrick's new shop and the house next door, which, I believe, they owned. My Uncle Jack (John Davies Thomas) now 101, tells me he attended the tin school. Owing to the sloping site, the back part was about 4ft higher than the front and I remember playing underneath it. (Mr Arthur Jones, 1997)

The temporary Machen Tin School. Few inhabitants today can remember its existence.

The official opening of school on 11 January 1909. Among the local dignatories were Dr B.O. Barnard, Mr W.H. Davies, Mr G.D. Inkin and Miss A. Williams. Mr Inkin's original staff consisted of Miss J.A.C. Henney, Evan Lloyd, Edith and Henrietta Jones, later joined by Miss Alma Gimblett.

Classroom, showing gallery. Desks were placed on a raised area with steps to enable the teacher to see the children more easily.

Alfred Rogers, with horses and gambo outside the school. Note the number of chimneys required in addition to the 'heating apparatus'.

Although the accommodation was vastly superior to the old school, there were problems, as noted in the following log book extracts, particularly when rooms were hired for outside events which proved detrimental to cleanliness.

'Problems experienced with heating. The central hall was used in the hope of getting the over 5's who are in the north classrooms to feel warm. Fires had to be lit in addition to the heating apparatus and oil lamps were used to bring up the warmth.'

'The atmosphere of the room is excessively nauseating this morning. Miss Williams (the governess) opens all windows, doors and every ventilator. Does not improve as the floor is saturated with brown spit-stains from which the offensive effluvia of stale tobacco etc., is arising. Room used for political meeting.'

A group of older girls with the headmistress, outside the old school at Glan-yr-Afon in the early twentieth century.

Miss A. Williams, (the headmistress or 'Governess') and Miss B. Henney with infants, outside the Infants' School (the church hall).

It was in 1902 that the pit at Nine Mile Point was sunk and aptly named Coronation Colliery. This pit, together with Risca colliery, became the workplace of many Machen men who made their way over the moutain in all weathers, their welfare receiving scant consideration.

My father worked at Nine Mile Point, I've been over the mountain with him more than once. He had an accident and hurt his back – no doctors at the pit in those days. They put him on a donkey and brought him home. Just imagine what he must have gone through; the donkeys on the beach at Barry Island were bad enough! (Fred Buckley)

My grandfather, when he was putting his food in his tommy tin to go down the pit, always put his sandwiches etc. in, and also a piece of crust. I asked him what was the crust for, and he said 'that's my thumbit. Our hands are so dirty with coal dust that we use that to wrap round them, and hold that, and our sandwiches keep clean'. My brother-in-law said that was done on the farm as well. The tommy tins were rounded one end, straight at the other end with a handle on the top. They put the round end down in their pocket first. (Mrs M. Jeremiah)

The two brick houses at the top of Church Street, always known as The Croft, were also built in 1902, and it has recently been discovered that they were also originally named Coronation Cottages to commemorate the accession of Edward VII.

The Pandy Mill was still operating, having been taken over around 1900 by the Jones family from Llandysul, one of the well-known flannel making villages of Cardiganshire (now Dyfed). No doubt they came with high hopes, since they had several girls working for them who followed them down from Cardiganshire, but the Pandy did not flourish and the company was eventually wound up in 1904.

The original plaque on the Croft, built on the site of a thatched cottage of the same name.

A family named Jones came to live at the Pandy, they were flannel weavers, and a number of local girls were employed. They had a little daughter, Eluned, and three sons, John Owen Jones, Gwilym Ifan and Daniel Arthur, all of them weavers. John Owen used to collect 6d a week for the flannel club, but later went into the ministry. He married Miss Lily Thomas of Nantygleisiad farm. (Mrs A. Edmunds)

The wealthy people for miles around would visit the Pandy with the approach of Christmas, and seek a pattern for materials they wanted. The Tredegar family were the best patrons, and I have pleasant memories of the treats that used to be prepared for us at Christmas when Lord Tredegar saw that every farm was well supplied with good cheer for the festive season. (Mrs R. Howells)

The Waterloo tin works was in full swing, and my Aunt Ann, who had a badly deformed right foot and left hand, was taught to use a treadle sewing machine by which she was able to earn a comfortable living – though some never paid. Mrs Jones from the Pandy used to bring a roll of flannel to our cottage and a pattern of a "short shirt" which the mill men used for working. My aunt had a regular order for the shirts, for which she charged 1s 3d, and Mrs Jones always collected the money and paid it over to my aunt.

The tin works registered as a new private company in 1902, entitled The Waterloo Tinplate Works. One of the directors was John Paton, a metal merchant from Pontypool, who was connected with the 'Waterloo' for many years.

Machen was still lit by candles and oil lamps, with entertainment largely dependent on church and chapel. This reminiscence of a Methodist gathering sets the scene very vividly.

The torchlight procession was a great attraction. Everybody taking part arrived at the meeting place, Brynteg, near White Hart, carrying a candle in a jam-pot, bulls-eye lantern or a lantern borrowed from Machen Brecon and Merthyr Station which could show three different coloured lights by the turning of a handle. We would halt at the conker tree, and others joined us on the way down to the Methodist church in Chatham. The circuit minister carried a torch which was a bundle of sacking soaked in paraffin oil.

Penny Readings were held in Adullam or Capel-y-Groes. The Revd D. Lloyd Williams was the minister of Adullam and a great help to the children. The Rechabite tent met in Siloam vestry and gave some lovely tea parties. The Band of Hope met in Siloam too. Robert Jones was Band of Hope leader; we all called him Bob and he was a good pal. We had a most interesting and enjoyable childhood – we were on big happy family. (Mrs A. Edmunds)

The Revd C.E.T. Griffiths succeeded the Revd J.C.S. Darby, remaining in the parish until 1913. His wife started the Girls Friendly Society, which became very popular.

We held a Tulip Fair, when we dressed in blue dresses, Dutch bonnet and fichu. Then we performed 'The Honour' in fancy dress and gave a tableau display. Mrs Hardy took charge of the choruses and for the Autumn Tableau sang 'Coming through the Rye'. Mrs Griffiths organised the first fruit and vegetable flower show to be held in Machen, and we had it down at Lower Machen in the big field behind school house. My parents won several prizes. There was also a prize for the best-kept cottage, and an old lady who lived in the cottage near the Hollybush won it. She had scrubbed the handle of her sweeping brush and put it to stand by the door. (Mrs A. Edmunds)

Adullam was the Congregation chapel, demolished in 1970. Capel-y-Groes, the Calvinistic Methodist Chapel is now a private dwelling next to Machen Rugby Club.

Draethen Village in the early twentieth century, viewed from the Holly Bush with Toll House, long since demolished.

The Lewis's Arms was very popular at this time, and had been run by the Haines family for several decades, to be followed by H.C. Bowden in 1901. Joseph Haines had a niece with a good memory!

Joseph Haines was landlord of the Lewis's Arms and did lots of trade. He had an excellent helper in his niece Laura Haines (Mrs Walter Woodruff), who prided herself in knowing the Christian name of every child and what shift the father was on. If children were a bit shy she could always produce a juicy pear, an apple, or two Victoria plums, of which there was an abundant crop in the Lewis's Arms orchard. That very soon gave the information required. She also kept the score for Joe.

(The 'score' was either adding up 'the slate' – men would have a pint and put it on the slate until pay-day – or the skittle alley had a flourishing team for many years; possibly she kept the skittle score!)

The Bowdens had three boys and a girl. Horace Bowden, the youngest son, owned a magic lantern, which was new to us and sent pears, Victoria plums and almost everything else into the background. We always asked lots of girls and boys to come to see the lantern, which Horace operated in the big wash-house at the back of our cottage. Mrs Bowden was good to all the boys and girls and gave her daughter Mildred a glorious birthday party every year to which we were all invited.

The 'Club Feast' was held yearly at the Lewis's in connection with the members of the R.A.O.B. (Royal Ancient Order of Buffaloes). We had a large brick oven, in which my mother roasted all the joints for the feast: beef, mutton, pork and a goose or two. These were served with roasted or mashed potatoes, and lots of lovely good hot gravy. There was rice pudding or plum duff to finish off, and the men had one drink before leaving – the cider was very good. (Mrs A. Edmunds)

The Lewis's Hotel, and its proprietor H.C.
Bowden, in the early twentieth century.

Advertisement from Trade Directory of 1901.

47

The village grocery shop in Commercial Road, run for many years by Evan Jones, is shown in the framed photograph (right). These family heirlooms date from the mid-1870s. Evan Jones's descendants have a stick engraved with his name and dated 1887 which was presented to him by the wholesalers he dealt with. The business was later run by Miss Stephens as an ironmonger's shop.

By 1906 the village had a branch of the Newport Co-operative Industrial Society, in addition to several other grocers, drapers, a butcher, a milliner, and a Mrs Sarah Ann Evans, who was a boot and shoe-maker, not to mention other small shops trading in the front rooms of houses.

Richard Davies of Craig-y-Rhacca farm, delivered milk each morning, and there was always plenty of milk at John Stephen, Ysgubor Fach farm, and at Bovil farm where Mr Little lived, and fresh warm milk at a penny a pint from Samuel Davies, Dranllwyn. We loved fetching the milk, as we were always given a glass full to drink.

The river was famous for lovely trout, and most Machen men could fish. Night lines were often used, and the night shift coming home early next morning would gather the lines and a lovely lot of trout would be cleaned and cooked for breakfast. (Mrs A. Edmunds)

One of the village characters in those days was Dr Benjamin Osmond Barnard who came to Machen at the end of the nineteenth century. He was a member of the school board, and took an active part in village activities. He lived for many years at 1 Doctor's Row on Commercial Road, before moving to Le Vallon opposite, which was built in the early twentieth century by William Henry John of Park farm, Lower Machen, who was also the village butcher.

There was Dr Barnard and a Dr Mackenzie of Caerphilly, who visited his own surgery in Church Street twice weekly. Both doctors were on the best of terms and never seemed to mind people making good use of them both, often at the same time. People left Barnard sometimes, and would soon let him know the medicine of Dr Mackenzie had done them more good. He always replied 'Carry on with Mackenzie; he can use a good whip on a tired horse'. (Mrs A. Edmunds)

Dr Barnard's time in Machen encompassed the age of the horse and trap and the motor car. He was a little man and suffered a great deal from gout, and his fingers looked like a bunch of small over-ripe bananas. His treatment for his gout was home-produced. There was an orchard at the back of his house, and he used to collect windfalls which had begun to rot, and he would take these as a sort of medicine, and I think that, without knowing it, he had found penicillin. (Russell Harris)

The village post office and stores, known today as The Old Post, provided Mrs Alice Edmunds with her first job.

I left school before I was twelve to commence my first job at the local post office as a learner, which meant learning the Morse code and counter work. I was at the post office for fifteen years. Telegrams were sent and received by Morse by means of the Needle, which was a box affair screwed to the counter and operated by the pressing of a stud sending out dots and dashes to Newport Head post office. Later on, the Needle was removed and a brass sounder in a bonnet-shaped cover with a brass key screwed to a small tablet was used. This was an improvement on the needle.

The first telephone exchange under the National Telephone Scheme was installed at a milliner's shop in Lewis Street kept by Mrs Martha Davies. The switch-board was screwed to the wall of her sitting room, and the "silence cabinet" installed in the shop. The post office took over telephones in 1912, and the switch-board and cabinet were brought into Machen post office. Mail was delivered twice daily, and the Sunday mail was brought up by a town postman on a push bike, the office being open from 8 a.m. until 10 a.m. Prior to that arrangement, a man by the name of Morgan John Morgan, who lived in a wooden hut just below Church Road station in Lower Machen, used to carry the mail to and from Newport. James Everson was appointed town postman; Walter John Howells, Weavers Row, Auxiliary; and Jane Ann Anthony, Chatham Delivery, became the first woman to wear the post office uniform. (Mrs A. Edmunds)

Machen was slowly acquiring the trappings of a small town, yet the feudal influence of the Tredegar estate was still very much in evidence.

The old post office, Upper Machen.

The Tredegar Hunt leaving the Holly Bush in more recent times, led by Bert Molyneux, Master of the Hounds. Onlookers include Alec Jones, Ron James, Arthur Joseph and Frank Donald. A yearly Balaclava dinner was held here for all estate employees.

I well remember Colonel Morgan, Ruperra Castle, arriving at the parish church (St Michael's) on Sunday mornings, where he would be brought by a coachman, carriage and pair of greys. The castle maids who attended service walked by way of the castle woods. All were dressed alike in black bonnets and cloaks, and stood outside the church door on either side of the path until he arrived; then they would follow him into the church. (Mrs A. Edmunds)

Colonel Frederick Morgan took part in the battles of Alma, Sebastopol, and Balaclava, and was MP from 1874 to 1906. He was a fine horseman, hunting regularly at Ruperra, but suffered in later life from lumbago, which he referred to as 'lumbugger'! He died in 1909.

Fashion was also changing. Styles became simpler, the crinoline and bustle had disappeared, and skirts which fitted smoothly over the hips, widening out towards the bottom became the order of the day, together with tight fitting blouses and larger sleeves. Sleeves became bigger and bigger, and were nicknamed 'leg of mutton' style. As Edward VII's short reign progressed, the bicycle was becoming popular. Motor cars began to appear, although few had the money or inclination to make them commonplace, but this also influenced fashion to quite a degree. The bell-shaped skirt was fashionable until about 1908, and then the 'hobble skirt' arrived. Older folk still wore bonnets and shawls, and usually dressed in black, while young girls were attracted to large hats, often heavily trimmed with flowers, feathers or ribbons. Working clothes for women in the home usually consisted of long skirts and blouses. Chapel anniversaries, Easter and Whitsun festivals were regarded as times for new hats, and with sixteen dressmakers in the village together with shops stocking materials, outfits could be obtained easily, provided they could be afforded.

A portrait of the Everson family from New Row. From left to right, front row: Amy Everson, John Everson Snr, John Everson Jnr, Mary Everson, Melvin Everson. Jim Everson is at the back of the group.

Wesley Hill, showing the end of the Yard buildings on the far right. Opposite, is the barn Tom Davies used for his carpentry and undertaker's business. The road narrowed after passing the entry to the Run, which is just out of picture on the right.

Top left: Tal Edmunds, in velvet suit complete with buttonhole, with a faithful pal.
Top right: Old thatched cottage in Church Street, with Hannah (Granny) Sainsbury.

Group of stewards at the Agricultural Show in Lower Machen, with Major Davies of Machen House, Matt Matthews, Jack John, W. Beeston, Bert Beeston, W. Webb, ? Gratton, ? Sanders, T. Young, G. Beeston, Miss P. Stratton and Angus McKinnon (head gardener at Ruperra Castle).

Three smart lads in their best suits, Wesley Buildings in the background.

Above left: Mr and Mrs Cornelius Roberts in best attire. Mr Roberts farmed Ty Canol, and was also licensee of the Fwrrwm Ishta at one time.
Above right: Mrs Elizabeth Harris, who later ran a grocery and sweet shop in Commercial Road, beloved of many youngsters for its variety of goodies.

Members of the Trew family and a cottage at Draethen, in the early twentieth century.

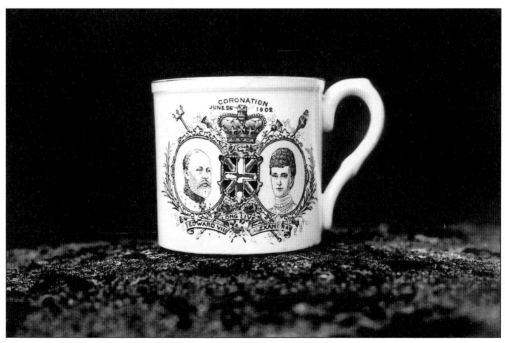

Coronation mug depicting Edward VII and Queen Alexandra, 1902.

Four

The First World War and Depression

George V was crowned on 22 June 1911, and the children at Machen school were given a holiday when he and Queen Mary visited Caerphilly the following year. At this time, the suffragette movement was gaining momentum, Captain Scott's journey to the South Pole, and the maiden voyage of the Titanic had both ended in tragedy, while in the nearby Aber Valley, the Senghenydd mining disaster had occurred with the appalling loss of 439 lives.

From 1894, when Risca Urban District was formed, Machen, together with Bedwas, became part of the new Magor and St Mellons Rural District Council, but 1912 saw the inauguration of Bedwas and Machen UDC consisting of twelve members, four from each of the Maesycymmer, Bedwas and Machen wards. The foundation stone of the council offices at Bedwas was laid on 1 July 1914.

Machen junior and infant schools were now well established in the building opened officially in 1909, although the original school at Glan-yr-Afon continued for a short time. The establishment of the Boy Scout movement in 1908 inspired one of the staff from west Wales to set up a troop in school.

By 1912 Mr Lloyd started a Boy Scout troop at Machen. He was thought to be consumptive and lived in a bell tent in the Vedw woods during the summers. He was a fine teacher and dedicated scoutmaster. The troop went away for summer camps. (Mr A. Jones)

A group of councillors shown at the foundation stone-laying ceremony at Bedwas, 1 July 1914.

A selection of log book entries in 1913 shows the new school to be very much part of village life:

'13 March: the managers have decided to close the school for tomorrow – Friday – the date of the funeral of the late Lord Tredegar. A large number of people from this district intend going to Bassaleg to view the same.

16 May: school closed this afternoon to enable children to attend Sanger's circus at Caerphilly.

13 June: the attendance is seriously affected by the exclusion of children suffering from tuberculosis. Rumours are abroad that members of the teaching staff are suffering from this disease and this must necessarily have a bad effect upon the school. (Whether this was connected with Mr Lloyd is not mentioned.)

17 November: the school closed today on the instruction of Dr Rocyn Jones who visited the school about 8 a.m. and declared it unfit for the assembly of children because the building was used for a pigeon show on Saturday. He has ordered the disinfection of same by the sanitary inspector.'

War

The everyday tenor of village life was shattered by the events in Europe which led to the declaration of war on 4 August 1914, and the carnage that ensued.

One of my mother's memories was of the outbreak of the First World War. This was announced at an annual fair at Rudry. The band stopped playing the music whilst it was announced, everything went soft and all went home. (Mrs B. Phillips Epsom)

Many Machen lads immediately volunteered for service and served in France and the Dardanelles, a far cry from the mountains of Machen, although one reminiscence shows that even in those days, the world could be a small place.

My cousin, Albert Vines, and a few Machen boys enlisted, and were sent to the barracks in Brecon. He managed to let us know that they would be leaving from there by train late at night. A great many of us gathered in the field at the end of Wyndham Street to wait for the train going past and wave them goodbye. (Muriel Phillips).

They embarked for France, eventually sailing from Marseilles to Greece where the South Wales Borderers were engaged in fighting the Turks in Salonika.

My grandfather served both on the Somme and at Ypres. Once he was driving an ambulance to the front line to pick up wounded. He arrived at the tent where the nurse told him off because he was very late. He replied saying he was sent out late and got lost, and asked for the chap he had to pick up. A voice came from inside the tent and said 'Yes, I might have guessed. Of all the people they could have sent to pick me up, it had to be Bertie Tamplin.' It was actually his next door neighbour from the Waterloo, Ebba Bounds. They lived next door to each other until my grandfather died in 1949. (Liz Phillips)

Dad used to tell the story how one morning, near Albert in France, he and Emmy Everson were in a party assisting in laying out bodies for burial. Amongst the bodies was Albert Vines (Luvvy). Suddenly, Emmy said 'Luvvy isn't dead'. A medical orderly was called and Luvvy was taken to hospital. He lived for many years after the war – his wife was Dolly Minty. (Eric Coleman)

The dreadful conditions endured by those in the theatres of war, although more fully realised today, could hardly have been envisaged by many at home, although efforts were made to help the wounded when they were recuperating.

I so vividly remember some Saturdays when Machen held fetes in the schoolyard for wounded and maimed soldiers, providing tea and entertainment. It was anguishing to watch so many with crutches and men with heavy head bandages who were blind, being led about. When tea was over, they listened enraptured to the school chorus singing 'Idle days in summertime' and the Welsh national anthem. The young ladies of the village were also invited to school to entertain them at tea parties held in the schoolyard. (Mr L. Salathiel)

Edmund (Emmy) Everson and John Coleman and in Salonika.

Wounded soldiers being encouraged to join in a hat trimming game, in the field in front of St John's church.

The signing of the Armistice in November 1918 brought peace, and although years of depression and unemployment were to follow, alongside came vast improvements in the provision of education and social amenities. Secondary education at this time was not available for all, but the old established Magor and St Mellons scholarships allowed some

War time photograph, 1915. From left to right, back row: Hilda Thomas, Harry Voyce, Harold Partridge, Billy Rees, Emlyn Moses, ? Hiscocks, -?-, Ronald Richards, Raymond Brown, Herbert Hicks, Mr G.D. Inkin. Third row: Eva Lewis, Sarah Bennett, Beryl Smith, Olwen Green, Olive Lewis, Lydia Shaw (Belgian refugee), Nellie Rees, -?-, Beryl Spargo. Second row: Lena Napier, Margaret Cook, Edna Griffiths, Mary Rees, Hilda Jones, Alice Harris, Daisy Rosser, Elsie Davies. Front row: Dick Maddocks, Garnon Williams, Ben Jones, Bill Harris, Hubert Thomas, Phillip Trew, Ivor Willans, Harold Hiscocks, Sam Hiscocks.

Mr G.D. Inkin, with his staff in 1915. From left to right: Anita Stephens (Beeston), Hilda Stephen (Davies), Hilda Thomas, Edith Everson (Jones), Alma Gimblett.

children to progress to higher education. Mr Inkin regularly entered pupils for the Newport Intermediate school (later to become Newport High school) with noticeable success, as already mentioned. Children had to achieve a certain standard before they could leave school at the age of thirteen and received a certificate to this effect.

School class, 1925. From left to right, back row: -?-, Daisy Williams, Hazel Perkins, Tommy Rosser, -?-, Deborah Burton, Marshall Price. Third row: Provy Morgan, Eddie Jones, Courtney Credgington, Johnny Moses, Ken Harrington, Phyllis Bristow, Gwyneth Holland, Bill Norman. Second row: Gordon Cook, Owen Jenkins, Albert Rodway, Iris Rogers, Susan Johns, Edna Hucker, Mair Jenkins, Eric Coleman. Front row: Tony Jones, Lovell Hill, Sybil Rowlands, Florence Griffith, John Stephens, Cyrus Hughes, Ray Davies.

Miss Griffiths, with mid-1920s class. From left to right, back row: Dorothy Everson, Trixie French, Muriel Williams, Gwen Richards, Iris Brown, Violet Matthews, Myra Ferris, Harry Richardson. Middle row: Betty Bristow, Mildred Price, Marie Harris, Betty John, Lenore Hughes, Ivor Moses, Russell Harris, Gwyn Willets. Front row: Wilf Howells, -?-, Arthur Edmunds, ? Salathiel, Ivor Green, Noel Harris, David Price, Trevor Davies.

Machen School Rugby Team, 1935/36. From left to right, back row: -?-, Wilf Hawkins, Arthur Minty, Frank Buckley, -?-, Victor Pope, Trevor Jones. Middle row: -?-, Alec Rees, Mr B.A. Williams, Lovell Hill, Mr E. Llewellyn, Eric FitzGerald, Milwyn Moses. Front row: Fred Phillips, Ralph Jones, Cliff Bowen.

Mid-1920s class. From left to right, back row: Raymond Everson, -?-, Billy Green, Wyndham Rogers, Selwyn Moses, Leolin Anthony, Norman Heath, Eddie Price, Alban Davies, Les Davies. Fourth row: Miss Phillips, Kitty Moses, Kathleen Howells, Margaret Escott, Mary Bowden, Clarice Rodway, Marjory Kew, Florence Hicks, Beryl Davies, Gladys Edwards. Third row: Daphne Righton, Connie Jones, Mary Buckley, Lenore Hughes, Rene Jones, Fanny Rogers, Gwyneth Moses, Myra Ferris, Gwen Watkins, Mr G.D. Inkin. Second row: Albert Watson, Wilf Pentecost, John Jones, Howard Matthew, Gwyn Willetts, Billy Thomas, Fred Cousins. Front row: Aubrey Pope, Billy Johns, Wilfred Harris, Arthur Edmunds, Harold Rees, Jackie Moses.

Mid-1920s class. From left to right, back row: Miss Heard, May Buckley, Ivy Green, Joyce Bane, Christina Perkins, Gwyneth Trew, Dorothy Rosser, Lilian Phillips, Annwyn Combes, Joyce Hawkins. Fourth row: Stella Hill, Violet Rogers, Elsie Hiscox, Muriel Bisset, Barbara Williams, Evelyn Everson, Olive Voyce, Rachel Davies, Irene Lwellyn, Peggy Matthews, Mr G.D. Inkin. Third row: Ernest Rees, Rual Davies, Norah Willetts, Doris Bryant, Rita Credgington, Nellie Evans, Phyllis Voyce, Raymond Cook, Fred Pope, Harold Matthews. Second row: Jack Williams, Donald Morgan, William Hicks, Alan Rodway, Gus Howells, Douglas Thomas, Charles Minty, Sidney Hurley. Front Row: William Banfield, Arthur Phillips, John Gimlett, Theo Evans.

In 1918 the school leaving age was raised to fourteen, and this gave impetus to the building of secondary schools. In the early 1920s, Machen children were going by train to Maes-y-Cymmer, to Caerphilly, the Lewis's school at Pengam and Newport High school. Bassaleg Grammar school was not built until 1935; pupils of secondary age were for some while accommodated in Rhiwderin.

The school staff had been joined by Mr J.T. Spinks and Mr Emrys Llewellyn in 1919 and 1922 respectively, and until the arrival of Mr B.A. Williams in 1931, the school played soccer. He introduced rugby shortly afterwards.

Amenities, taken for granted now, were still very medieval in the pre-war and post-war eras.

Earth closets were still the order of the day and were mainly outdoor and often communal. There was a periodic nightly collection of excrement by the night cart (most usually known as night soil). It was criminally unhygienic to have the deposit area for this material on what we called 'the ash tip' in close proximity to the old yellow brick school at Glan-yr-Afon. This ended soon after the First World War. (Malcolm Harris)

I remember our grandfather's funeral which was in January, and being wintertime, the lane was frozen up. There were no cars or hearse or anything, and the fashion was to carry the coffin to the church or chapel, and the bearers used to have a rest somewhere along the way. So, as you know, only coal fires were about then so everyone in the New Row had to keep their ashes every day, and riddle them on the lane ready for the funeral bearers to be able to take the coffin down the lane. The lane from New Row to the bridge was always known as the Ash Path because it was made up of coal dust and ashes from the old pit. (Mrs E. Fisher, née Rodway)

The main road and the more important side streets were lit by widely dispersed oil lamps. Few houses had an internal water supply. There were communal exterior water taps and a plentiful supply of street taps, with here and there, horse water troughs. There was the Cwm reservoir, and that apart, there were just the local wells and springs like the spout up at Nantygleisiad. Machen was still in the age of the horse and cart, and roads were all surfaced with gravel to accommodate the horses' hooves because of the steep inclines. (Russell Harris)

George Haskins in his horse and trap, adjacent to his home Forge Cottage and the viaduct.

The beginning of the break up of the Tredegar estate with the sale of cottages and dwellings took place on 26 June 1920. Seven cottages adjacent to Nantyglesiad chapel house with its adjoining buildings; the whole of Colliers' Row; cottages near the Forge Hammer; and the cottages in the Square at Church Street, together with the old Dranllwyn Cottage, went under the auctioneer's hammer at the King's Head in Newport.

The sale details for the cottages show that all had a piece of ground, some had orcharding, together with a pigscot and outside closet. Inside were bedrooms, living rooms, back kitchens with larder or pantry, but no baths or inside toilets. The particulars for Colliers' Row indicate that six or seven tenants shared the use of the communal bakehouses, and that the outside privies were jointly shared. Rents ranged from 8s to 15s per month for the terraced cottages, while semi-detached cottages rated a little higher at £1 to £1 5s per month. Many tenants were able to take the opportunity to buy their homes, which was a great step forward, at prices ranging from £150 to £200.

The 1920s saw great strides in the provision of a decent water supply, with the formation of the Rhymney Valley Water Board in 1921, who were responsible for bulk supply from the Taf Fechan Reservoir. This was to be followed by a main electricity supply in 1925. In addition to this, the Bedwas and Machen UDC set about improving housing and transport.

Much laughter and some excitement has been occasioned by the opening of the new council houses to prospective tenants. The village is a scene of great activity, furniture passing through the streets from morning till night, while the moving proceeds. Twenty-four of the forty houses have been completed, and it is anticipated that the remaining number will be finished in the near future. The houses occupy a site immediately above the station. They are built in two rows, which have been named Sunnybank and Brynhyfryd Terraces respectively. They are let at a rental of 14s 3d weekly. The houses have every modern convenience. They are twelve to the acre and are semi-detached, while many labour-saving devices are provided. Councillor E.B. James, who is Machen's representative on the Housing Committee, has taken a great interest in the housing problem, and credit is due to him. (Argus, 27 August 1927)

Ruperra. Estate workers and domestic staff in front of the summer house – a well-loved viewing point for all of us who used to walk to the castle.

Machen in the early 1930s, showing modern housing (mentioned above) provided by the Bedwas and Machen UDC.

The council instigated a regular bus service in 1922. A complete renovation of one such bus in those days, undertaken by a coach-builder and a coach-painter, cost twenty nine guineas!

Machen's pride was its railway network, provided by the Rhymney Railway and the Brecon and Merthyr Railway. The merger between the B & M and the Great Western Railway took place in 1922, and relations were a little strained in the early days!

My father (John Coleman) told me this story several times. When the GWR acquired the old B & M railway, the branch line to Caerphilly was two way working, and Machen Junction was important enough to have a full time shunter at the station. Initially, the GWR locos were not suited to the inclines they encountered on the B & M track. On at least one occasion, a GWR train working from Caerphilly to Machen failed to make the gradient from the viaduct to Machen station. The station-master ordered the shunter to go to its assistance, but the shunter refused point blank to do so. As a compromise the shunter agreed that if the GWR loco left the train, and climbed to the station alone, he would go down the branch and haul the train up. Once this was done, the shunter took the loco to the train and coupled up. Being of the old school of drivers who talked to his loco, he caressed the controls and muttered "come on, me lad, don't let me down, let's show the bugger how it should be done" and promptly hauled the train up through to the Vedw sidings. (Clive Coleman)

Machen had direct connections with Newport, Caerphilly, Pontypridd, Merthyr and Brecon. It was only if you wanted to get to Cardiff that you were required to make a change at Caerphilly. The service to Brecon ran via Bargoed, with a steep climb up to Beacon top, and then the descent into Brecon. There was also an express to Merthyr stopping only at Machen, Caerphilly, and Pontypridd. It took eleven minutes from Newport to Machen. This express ran twice a day in both directions. There was the local motor service between Machen and Caerphilly. Machen in those days was really a busy little rail junction. (Russell Harris)

Machen station in the days of steam, showing footbridge across the line and absence of housing, pre-1927.

Alongside modernisation of services and housing, came changes for the Machen work force. Mining in the village was confined to the old pit adjacent to Green Row, which had re-opened in the early twentieth century, and was still working for a few years in the early 1920s.

My father came here to re-open the old pit with Mr Morgan, I am almost certain it was Roy Morgan's father. Now in my nostrils is the smell of linseed oil. My father had a sort of bonnet hat with a huge brim like the top of a pouffee, and that piece round there was made with linseed oil and some other material. When I was a little boy he told me that he wore it when he was going down the shaft in a bogie, to clear the shaft. Often, it was full of water, dogs, cats, you name it! The hat was to stop the water from the shaft hitting his head. My father, up until the day he died, had the feeling that's how he lost his hair: through the cold water dropping on his head because they weren't in a cage; they were in an open bogie. They couldn't work from a cage because there were gutters round the shaft. (Emlyn Jones)

I can remember the old pit by the river working very well. My father was a pitman there, and I have stood many a time alongside the winder. The winding engine man would sit and wind the pit gear, and my father had to work on the top of the cage, inspecting the shaft to see if any repairs were needed to the stone or brickwork. They used to take the drams across the road as you go up to New Row, and to the tips behind the old Machen school. (Les Willetts)

Pentwyn drift mine also worked through the First World War, but was abandoned sometime in the 1920s.

Up in Pentwyn were the remains of the stand that was there for the motor to pull the drams up the incline. Les Morris, who is dead now, lived in Trethomas, and he was working for Mr Mitchell, the boss. They knew they were driving near the old workings of the pit, so they decided to go ahead, keep on and see what was there.

They made a hole, taking into consideration gas and all the rest. I can't remember his words exactly, but they put a lamp inside, and the iridescence shining inside there, because all the water coming from there was gold-coloured, was breath-taking. He said it was a most beautiful sight, the dramway was as good as ever, and there was a mandrel or shovel, whatever you want to call it, standing against the side. They touched it and it just evaporated into dust. Mitchell had another drift mine, and Trevor Hughes and several others worked for him. He lived in the Waterloo. (Emlyn Jones)

The opening of Bedwas Pit in 1912 when the first coal was raised, widened the employment prospects for many, in addition to the pits at Nine Mile Point, Pengam, Penallta and Risca, although it was a time of industrial strife.

A coal strike in 1921 was followed by the General Strike in 1926, and mining went through many years of depression in South Wales, owing to the high pricing of our currency abroad which made Welsh coal difficult to sell for export, where it had normally been in high demand.

While the miners' strike was on in 1921, it was not possible for the Waterloo to work as they relied on coal from Bedwas. It was then that the main sewer was laid down the valley through Machen, and many tin-plate workers (my father among them) took alternative work on that, not to be idle. (Liz Phillips)

'Excellent work is being done by the communal kitchen at Machen, (in the old school at Glan-yr-Afon) where meals are produced each day for about 150 men. There is no lack of willing helpers, and the local residents are subscribing liberally towards the expense of running the kitchen. All the concerts and entertainments arranged by the committee to raise money have been largely attended.' (Argus, 10 July 1926)

Willing helpers at the soup kitchen for unemployed miners set up in the old school by the river include Ethel Mary Haskins, Amy Everson and Mabel Williams.

I remember in those days the river was black and people would dig coal dust from the river. They would have a tin bath, and bore holes in it, then fill it with dust and the water would drain away through the holes. You would see them dragging the bath full of dust on pram wheels or something as far as Sunny Bank where I lived. Then they made it into balls, sometimes nine parts dust and one part cement, leave it for a week to set after putting the knife through it to cut into squares and it would burn terrific, burn the bottom out of the grate. There was always that smell, you were brought up with that. (Emlyn Jones)

It was on my mother's birthday that Mr Knight came to see us. My father spoke to him for some time, then he came back and said, 'I've got the best birthday present ever for your mother, I'm starting work on Monday.' I always remember that, there was such pleasure in our house; you just couldn't get over it. My Dad was going back to work in Bedwas Colliery. (Kath Panting)

The Waterloo Tinplate Works amalgamated with six other companies in 1921 and became known as Partridge Jones and John Paton Ltd. Although it continued working, it had periods of recession, closing for a while in 1927, and suffering short working weeks in the early 1930s, due to low demand.

One misfortune follows another at Machen. Following upon the removal of the GWR fitting shops to Caerphilly, the Waterloo Tinworks have closed. Although many men from the surrounding district were employed, Machen has been hit the hardest. It is estimated that about sixty men are thrown out of employment. (Argus, 16 April 1927)

I went to work in the Waterloo soon after I left school. Not mill work, but sweeping up. Cyril Hicks (who was later manager at the Co-op) had a very nasty gash on his hand, and straightaway they put me with Billy Morgan on No. 4 mill. Stan Partridge was working in No. 3 mill with Bill Rees, Mel Rees' brother, and Dai Rees was in No. 2 mill, the other side of the flywheel. No. 1 mill was Harry Harris from Top Row and a boy from Rudry, Griff Bale, was chucking up for him. Harold Llewellyn was chucking up for Dai Rees, Stan was chucking up for Bill Rees, and I was chucking up for Billy Morgan. We used to go in at 6 a.m., the shearer would come in at 7 a.m., so we had to go in to get so many sheets up on the bench ready for him to start at 7 a.m. Us boys had all done an hour's work

GWR engines in the repair shops before closure in 1927, which resulted in many families moving to the West Midlands where there were better job prospects. (NMGW Department of Industry)

Interior of the Waterloo Tin Works. (Dr A.E. Jukes).

Group of workers at the Waterloo.

before the shearer come in. I've seen me work there until 5 or 6 in the evening without a penny extra, well, in those days you were young, you did it. You couldn't go into the mills, into the white apron jobs until you were sixteen, that was night work, you see, but you could do, if there was what was called a catcher. There was a squad of six: the roller, the doubler, the first helper, the second helper, the furnace man and the behinder, we call them chuckers. Chucking up the sheets, they were long sheets, eight stuck together, and it was very heavy and hot work. I remember when I started I was so short, they put one of the flat boxes for me to stand on. (Les Willetts)

Two of the clocks used to time the pigeons' flights.

The Depression brought about the blossoming of home-made entertainment, which consisted of carnivals with decorated floats, jazz band competitions and fancy dress competitions, together with village concerts often held in different chapels. It was also popular at this time for people from Cardiff and Newport to visit the woods of Draethen and to climb Machen mountain on bank holidays. A favourite leisure time pursuit was the keeping of pigeons, and the racing of them.

My grandfather had pigeons when he was a young man, and the Voyces on Forge Road, Trevor Gimblett up Napier Street, and Bob Hill, Lovell Hill's father. They went to shows all over the place, many had racing pigeons. They used to take them down from Machen station to Newport station, register them and send them off by train, often to places in Scotland or the Shetlands. We used to know when the whimberries were out, my grandfather could tell by the pigeon droppings. He'd say 'whimberries are out, come on', and off we went up the mountain. (Les Brown)

Trevor Gimblett won three gold medals with his pigeons, and named his house 'Thurso'!

There was great rivalry among the pigeon owners. One of them made the comment that it was easy to win when you used the North Road (Scotland), so the winner took him up on it and took the South Road, racing his birds from France. He still won. (Clive Coleman)

'There was psychology in it too. Some of the men had hen birds, and they would race those birds because they would fly much faster in order to get back to hatch their eggs.' (Lloyd Davies)

It was in 1926, the year of the General Strike, that Revd Daniel Hughes, the minister of Siloam chapel and a man of exceptional gifts, arranged to take over the vestry of Siloam for recreational purposes. On the top floor he installed a full-sized billiard table and the Siloam Billiards Club was formed. He also had machinery installed for people to repair their shoes. In later years, classes were held for crafts and cookery.

Revd Daniel Hughes with committee members, Siloam Social Club. From left to right, back row: Mark Bristow, Charlie Bristow, Billy Rodway, Cllr Ted James, Lloyd Harris, Reg Minty, Ray Hicks. Middle row: Roy Bain, Will Jenkins, Stan Rosser, Ted Harris, Noel Davies, Harold Davies. Front row: Reg Young, Cyril Powell, Revd Daniel Hughes, Cyril Davies, Bill Powell.

Two contrasting portraits of Daniel Hughes: as county councillor, and in a dramatic portrayal of a scene from A *Tale of Two Cities*. He gave readings which were very popular, including A *Christmas Carol*, *Three Men in a Boat* and *All Quiet on the Western Front*. The latter was interspersed with his own experiences, which included the retreat from Mons in 1914. He also lectured for the WEA; adjudicated at Machen cultural events; and wrote the words for many Baptist hymns.

Nurse Margaret Thomas.

Many families in Machen after the First World War and throughout the 1920s and 1930s paid into a Sick Club, while some doctors set up their own schemes for those with families on low income. Then there was what was known as the 'Panel' which was for those who were able to pay when they visited the doctor.

Dr Barnard, who has already been mentioned, had several assistants: Dr MacSweeney was the first, being followed by Drs Davies and Morgan, both of whom married daughters of Mr W.H. Davies who owned a large shop in the village. Dr Morgan moved away while Dr Cecil Davies remained in the village, his surgery being situated in part of the shop later known as Russell House.

Dr Edith Davies, whose family came from Panteg farm in Lower Machen, was also practising in 1929 when there was a diphtheria epidemic in the village. Her surgery was in what is now known as the Top Club. The district midwife was also a much valued and respected member of the community. Two district nurses remembered affectionately by many still were Nurse Jenkins who lived in Forge Road, and Nurse Margaret Thomas who came to Machen in 1920.

Home-made remedies were often relied on, since the doctor was only called when there was a serious problem. Brimstone and treacle were usually administered once a week, elderflower tea or elder-blow as it was called, was a good standby, and Mrs Tonwen Cole in New Row could always supply dried elderflower for this purpose. Arrowroot was mixed into a paste, rather like custard, for stomach upsets, and vinegar and brown paper were used for headaches. A remedy for bronchitis or coughs was a trip on the train with the window wound down, so that the sulphur fumes could be inhaled. Sore throats were treated by camphorated oil or goose grease being rubbed on the chest, covered with an old piece of flannel. Senna pods and California syrup of figs were in common use for dealing with bowel problems, in later years to be followed by Ex-lax.

My grandmother, who lived in the White Hart, worked as the midwife in Machen. I am told she used to go round on a bike carrying her bowls and her buckets. She didn't trust anyone else with them. She waited until I was born, and Emlyn Jones was the next to be born, and he had to have the new midwife so I was the last of the line. (Mrs M. Jeremiah, née Rosser)

The visit of the school dentist was always followed by the giving out to many of the dreaded pink form. This meant a visit to the 'slaughter wagon', as we called it. My memory of the dentist was the use of the foot-operated drill when you needed a filling. It was not very pleasant! Loose teeth were pulled out with a piece of cotton, sometimes a coin was put under your pillow by the pixies or fairies if you hadn't made too much fuss. (Lloyd Davies and Doug Thomas)

Well-known social meeting places were set up in this era. The first of these, the Machen Working Men's Constitutional Club and Institute, was founded in 1921 and met in an old wooden army hut known as 'the Ark'.

Caerphilly Miners' Hospital with new entrance buildings, 1930. The chairman of the hospital committee at that time was Gwyn Morgan of Machen, who died shortly afterwards at the early age of thirty-two years. The hospital, which opened in 1923, was originally a large private residence, *The Beeches*. After its purchase, the conversion was funded by miners, each of whom paid 6d per week.

'The Ark', opposite the school, now demolished.

Beer like Lloyd's of Newport, Webbs of Aberbeeg and Rhymney's Taff Brew were served behind the bar. There were never any games in the bar on Sundays and, until 1938, women were not allowed. Among the regulars was a blind piano tuner, Mr Stan Gregory, who played cards with an ordinary pack. Unemployed people in Machen would get a joint of beef from the Institute every weekend. (Local unknown newspaper cutting)

Secondly, many Machen ex-servicemen who had been members of other local branches of the British Legion for some years, decided that a Machen branch should be formed. This was done at a meeting held at the Tredegar Arms on 15 October 1932. The first officers were Chairman Revd A.G.A. Picton, Vice-Chairman Mr A.M. Rees, Secretary Mr Cage and Treasurer Mr S. Hiscox. For the first few months, members met in the school before moving to the Co-op premises in Commercial Road, which were rented at 5s per week. During the early 1930s, much time was taken up with the establishment of fund-raising activities.

Nothing seems to have escaped the attention of the entertainments committee. There were whist drives, smoking concerts, rifle shooting, archery, darts, billiards, fancy dress, annual dinners, poultry drives, push ball competitions, and annual fetes, which catered for everyone. Stalls included goldfish, hoopla, pitch penny, pound stalls, fortune teller, treasure hunt, coconut stall and, of course, a tea stall and an ankle competition for the ladies. (Gerry Kingdon)

One of Machen's most valuable leisure facilities was created between 1928 and 1930, when Viscount Tredegar gave eight acres of ground to the Machen Recreation Welfare Association, which was formed with the objects of 'promoting the social well-being, recreation and conditions of living of workers in or about coal mines in the neighbourhood of Machen'. The Miners' Welfare Fund, which had been established in 1920, allocated £1400 for the purpose of laying out and equipping the land as a public recreation and pleasure ground. The area was laid out to provide for rugby football and baseball, together with a children's play area provided with large and substantial see-saws, each capable of holding several children each side, a variety of swings and a large roundabout. A wooden pavilion surrounded by a small lawn with a privet hedge, and a separate toilet building was also built.

Rugby team, 1929/30. From left to right, back row: R. Baynton, T. Fitzgerald, W. Griffiths, J. Davies, R. Davies, G. Vines, M. Pearce, H. Voyce, G. Evans, W.H. John, J.T. Morgan. Middle row: Trevor Williams, T. Young, I. Harris (vice-captain), L.T. Phillips (captain), F. Brown, R. Green, D. Owen. Front row: T. Voyce, A. Butler, P. Richards.

Machen school, during 1920s and 1930s, had seen the retirement of Miss Annie Williams who had served thirty-two years as the 'governess' and head teacher of the infants' school, and also of Miss Bessie Henney, in 1936, who had taught with her at the old school in the church hall. Miss Williams was succeeded by Miss P.G. Harris. The junior school continued under the headmastership of Mr G.D. Inkin.

The following photographs have been selected from this period.

Mr. Inkin at work with a scholarship group, which includes Alice Davies, Phyllis Prince, Beryl Price, Linda Bissett and Reg Dickinson.

Machen Infants School. From left to right, back row: -?-, -?-, Joan Watson, Anita Griffiths, Norman Jeremiah, Donald Button, Derek Cross, Barbara Hicks, Cynthia Greenhaf, Alan Morgan, Miss Harris (headmistress). Fourth row: Sadie Davies, Jimmy Sweetland, -?-, Glenys Rowles, Marjorie Thomas, -?-, Rita Williams, -?-, Doris Baynton, Dennis Hartley, -?-. Third row: Ray Davey, John Humphreys, Raymond Messenger, Percy Spooner, Eldon Gadd, Olive Rogers, Dennis Spargo, Don Harris, Ken Rogers. Second row: Brynmor Rowlands, Frank Gregory, Ron Johns, Ken Baynton, Avril Rogers, Mavis Hartley, -?-, Hilary Morgan, -?-. Front row: Dennis Harper, Roy Harris, Reggie Button, Cliff Baynton, Doris Bowen.

Machen school class, 1935-1936. From left to right, back row: Hiram Everson, -?-, Ken Holland, Lewis Richards, Alan Morgan, Dennis Spargo, Donald Budge, Clive Coleman. Third row: Mr J.T. Spinks, Derek Cross, Percy Heath, Donald Button, Wilfred Hawkins, Emrys Hicks, Arthur Minty, Idwal Watkins, Ron FitzGerald, Mr Emrys Llewelyn. Second row: Leslie Rowles, Jimmy Sweetland, Vincent Beacham, Ray Davey, Jaci Gooding, Roy Burnett, Don Jones, Wilfred Davey, Victor Pope, Ernest Jones. Front row: 'Snowy' Walters, Eric Credgington, Billy Dickinson, George Ellis, Stanley Ellis, Leslie Baynton, Brynmor Rowlands.

Machen Silver Jubilee Carnival, 1935. Mr J.H. Hufton leads the contingent from Machen Gymnastic Club.

The period between the First and Second World Wars in Machen was certainly a time of social deprivation, but alongside came social progress. Unemployment in 1932 was 2.75 million, and a 10% tariff was imposed on all imports, with concession for empire goods. The population of Machen remained steady, increasing by about a hundred between 1911 and 1931.

The King and Queen's Silver Jubilee celebrations took place in May 1935, and a celebration and sports day was held in Machen. Miss Gwladys Harris, head of the infant department in Machen school, offered to run an extra event to separate the infants from Standards 1 and 2, and donated 11s which covered the cost of three prizes for each of the two classes. The secretary of the sports committee was Mr A. Shapcott.

Mr G.D. Inkin in retirement, strolling down to the Recreation Ground.

Coronation Mug to commemorate the Coronation of George V and Queen Mary, 1911.

The end of an era for Machen and its school came that same year on 31 July, when an entry in the school log book recorded:

I complete my forty years active teaching service on 31 August and in accordance with the education committee's resolution, I retire on that day. This is my last day of active service, and I take this opportunity to thank the staff and all who have assisted me in conducting the school to the full satisfaction of those in authority. (G.D. Inkin)

Five
The Second World War
Peace and Recovery

Although the government had stated, shortly before the death of George V, that Britain had 80% recovered from the Depression, when his eldest son Edward VIII succeeded him in 1936, there was still great hardship for many without jobs. The Jarrow Hunger March begun in October, when miners from the North walked to London to plead their case, and were refused a hearing.

Edward VIII visited South Wales a few weeks later, where unemployment in Merthyr Vale had risen to over 50%. Many people had no option but to seek work in less depressed areas.

My husband related how his parents had taken him and his two brothers to London for the day. His dad worked on the railway and they had free passes. After visiting a Lyon's tea house, which was quite a treat, they came out to find some of the marchers were standing in the street. His dad straightaway put his hand in his pocket and gave them money. It made a great impression on him, so much so that he broke down once when he told me. He never forgot it. (Delphine Coleman)

The following entry from the school log book, made by Mr T.A. Bateman who succeeded Mr Inkin, needs no comment.

17 December 1936: distributed thirteen pairs of boots amongst the children of families in need. These proved very insufficient in dealing with eighty children of unemployed parents. Supplied editor of the Morning Post, London, with a list of ninety names of children attending this school whose parents had been unemployed for long periods. Each will receive a Christmas present.

Sadly, Mr Bateman was taken ill shortly afterwards, and died after an operation for appendicitis on 19 January 1937. He was succeeded by Mr J.T. Spinks.

On the 12 May 1937, following the abdication of Edward VIII, his younger brother, the Duke of York was crowned George VI, the event being the BBC's first outside television broadcast, although it was to be many years before Machen had the benefit of a local transmitter. Machen celebrated with a sports day and street tea parties. Each child was presented with a Coronation mug.

Sports and leisure activities, organised by enthusiasts within the village, were still part of everyday life, and support was wholehearted.

Machen Baseball Club, Argus Cup and Pontypridd Carnival Cup Winners in Coronation Year. From left to right, back row: T.R. FitzGerald, -?-, Tal Edmunds, C. Harris, Alban Davies, W. Adams, Ralph Morgan, Redvers Green, Edward Jones, E.T. Morgan, John Emy Everson. Middle row: H.D. Esterre Darby, Harold Harris, C. Ashman, Tommy Young, T. Crisp, P. Hynam, D.T. Newton Wade. Front row: Reg Young, Mel Everson.

Machen Rugby Club, 1936/37. From left to right, back row: Fred Rees (Patsy), Tom FitzGerald, Elvet Davies, Jim Everson, Ivor Harris, Arthur Thomas, Hubert Thomas. Third row: Allen Skuse, Bill Martin (chairman), John S. Thomas, Linc Everson, Arthur Bowden, William Richards (Billy Pandy), Redvers Green (Docker), Stan Thomas, I. Jenkins, Alec Griffiths, Charlie Harris (secretary), Dick Maddocks. Second row: A. Bennett (Teaky), S.J. Goldsworthy, Jack Davies (Shon), Alban Davies, Harold Harris, A. Kear. Front row: Ewart Martin, Ivor Davies (Dinky).

One of the great successes of Machen's leisure pursuits was the Machen Dramatic Society, which was formed in July 1936. Their enthusiasm was evident by the fact that they decided to enter two plays in the Monmouthshire Drama Festival that same year. From producing one act plays in the church hall, they progressed to full length plays, the first being 'The Passing of the Third floor Back', which they performed at Bedwas Hall to an audience of 800. After a break during the war, they were revived and, under the production expertise of Mrs N. Willis, went from strength to strength with regular full-length plays.

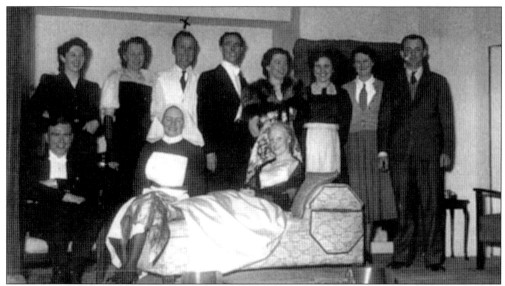

Machen Dramatic Society, *Miranda*, 1951. From left to right, back row: Mary Sharples, Alice Lewis, Clive Tamplin, Bill Panting, Beryl Drake, Kath Panting, Mary Oswell, Victor Drake. Front row: Elvet Roderick, Nellie Willis, Megan Baynton.

Machen Dramatic Society, *The Killer Dies Twice*, 1957. From left to right, back row: Harry Brusallis, Roy Morley, Josie Davies, Don Willis, Victor Drake. Front row: Alice Lewis, Kathleen Rosser, Marjorie Beavis.

War Returns

Within two years of the Coronation, events in Europe were moving towards the outbreak of another war, just as had occurred so soon after the crowning of George V. War was declared against Germany on 3 September 1939, and Machen was soon coping with ration books, petrol coupons, blackout restrictions, ARP and Home Guard duties, after seeing its young people off to the services, some never to return to their homes and families.

Class of evacuees, Machen, 1940. The group includes June Lawry, Jeanne Kirk, Josie Adams, Betty Hyland, Beryl Reid, Miss Edmunds, Molly York, Doreen Bowman, Gladys Foster, Jean Norman, Audrey Norman, Nora Thompson, Joyce Thompson, Maureen Cooper and Doreen Gillard.

Mr and Mrs E.W. Jones outside Buckingham Palace on 29 October 1946, with the Military Medal awarded to their son, Trevor, of the South Wales Borderers. The award was announced several months prior to his death, but news of it never reached him, far away in Burma.

Above left: The Clark family: Vida, Roy with baby Frank, little Mary and Betty, together in Machen.
Above right: Haydn Askey and Jean Pitcher at the top of Alma Street.

Mr Spinks took up a commission in the forces in June 1940, and Mr Emrys Llewellyn was in charge at Machen school until his return, dealing with the arrival of some eighty young evacuees from Gillingham in Kent. They were all living close to the Naval Dockyard at Chatham, which was under imminent danger of attack. The authorities in charge of the evacuation gave families only two days in which to decide whether their children should be sent away. It was a heartbreaking choice for many mothers whose husbands were away in the services, while for the children, it was both exciting and traumatic.

I was ten when with my brother, Roy (eleven), and my sister, Vida (eight), we were evacuated to Machen. Alderman Tom Jones was the billeting officer. On arrival, I well remember seeing the slag heaps and cable buckets on top of the mountain, walking in a crocodile down from the station, wearing our luggage labels and boxed gas masks, holding my sister's hand and telling her not to worry. If she wanted anything, she must tell me: 'I'll make them understand'. Ladies stood at their front doors, babies wrapped in blankets, 'Welsh fashion', and one called 'Here come the refugees', and I thought, 'Oh good, they speak English'. Roy was in the church choir at Christmas, and sang the part of the page in Good King Wenceslas. I was so proud of him. (Miss B. Clark)

My parents had an evacuee lad, and he was a lovely boy. Although food was rationed, we always had a good table, and when Mam found out it was his birthday, she somehow managed to do something different. She did it as she always did for us all, but he couldn't get over it, and told us it was the first time he had ever had a birthday party. He came back to see us many years later. (Jane Wakeley)

I remember one lad who was rather overwhelmed by all the woods and trees around. We were near the river bridge by the Legion, and he said 'What time does the park shut?'. He didn't realise that the ash tip and the wood were places where we played whenever we wanted. (Clive Coleman)

My memories of Machen were that there was no electric light in the cottage where I was billeted, instead they used Valor lamps. Cooking was done on a range, there was a coal bunker at the back door, and always a pail of slack set beside for the fire. After school we changed and went to pick up wood for the fire which was dried in the oven. It was a strict rule never to rake out the ashes, they were the basis for the next day's fire.'

I remember watching the flashes in the sky from the cottage, and being very frightened. Mrs Jones were busy embroidering and told me, 'Don't worry, you'll go to God.' Another time we were chased by local children up the Crescent. They were throwing stones, and we got hold of dustbin lids and used them as shields. We had a good fight, but were strongly disciplined by Mr Llewellyn who must have heard about it. (Mrs C. Robbins née Neesam)

I can't remember the exact date, but I do know that it was the weekend of Dunkirk, as we were put into a siding so that a troop train could pass. We were told the soldiers had come from Dunkirk. We didn't, of course, know what that meant. I was allocated to a family called Minty: Mr George, Mrs Minnie and two girls, Margaret and Dorothy. We lived at Belle Vue house, Commercial Road, just a little way from the main village and opposite the recreation ground with the river between. I used to go to the post office each week to cash the postal order my mother sent me for pocket money. I remember there was a fish shop because when there was no fish available, which was most of the time, they used to make fritters of slices of potato dipped in batter. Sometimes they would put a slice of spam between two pieces of potato, dip the lot in batter and fry that. It sounds horrible now, but we loved it then. There were classes by the St John's Ambulance Brigade in junior first aid, home nursing and child welfare. They were well attended, and I still have the certificates which I gained there. I was confirmed in Lower Machen church in April 1943. (Mrs E. Tyrrell, née Whiffin)

Ethel Whiffin, with Dorothy and Margaret Minty, on the old roundabout 'down the rec', with the Vedw House in the background.

The Crescent, Machen, 1940, prior to the building of the British Legion, the village hall and Glan-yr-Afon.

I can't give you my address because I don't know where I am. I think it's at a place called Rude Herring, (Rhiwderin) at least that's what it sounded like. Five of us were collected by Mrs Griffiths and taken to Machen House. As we drove up the drive, we were all speechless, all except Johnny who kept muttering, 'Bloody hell, bloody hell'. The front lawn is so big, you could get two football pitches into it, and there's a tennis court and two lakes with a rowing boat and a pigsty and lots of garages and buildings, a stream and a fish pond. (Mr M. Haisman)

We were housed with Mr.Wilfred and Mrs.Annie Bodrell. We used to go for summer picnics on Machen mountain and collect whimberries, and go sledging in the winter on the slopes. We had to learn the Welsh national anthem word perfect, which I still remember very well. We went to chapel Sunday morning, afternoon and most Sunday evenings to the Ebenezer. Mrs.Bodrell was a very good cook, I enjoyed my meals and her fruit cake. (Mrs D. Cook, née Gillard)

In addition to the evacuees, men from India and Holland came to Machen and were billeted at Ruperra.

When the Indians came to Ruperra castle, they arrived at Machen station. There must have been about 150 to 200 men, and they off loaded the horses from their boxes into the old coal yard. There was a gate there, as one went up to the station. You went over the bridge and on the left were the railings towards the coal yard. We came down from the bridge to watch these beautiful horses. All of a sudden, the train blew its whistle, and one of the horses bolted, dragging one of the soldiers and he fell down. The horse went to jump the gate, and the spikes on the top went into its stomach, so they had to destroy it straight away. (Les Brown)

83

The Dutch soldiers, or Netherlanders, arrived at Ruperra in the early 1940s. We, as children in Draethen, were agog to see probably the first foreign people in our lives. They spoke a very different language, and we could not understand them, yet there were some words we had heard somewhere before, could it be Welsh? Evidently, when they first arrived in Britain, after escaping from the Germans, they landed in Milford Haven and were received by a Welsh speaking population. They thought they were learning English from these people, but in fact it was Welsh. On arrival at Ruperra they had to start learning English again.

Early in the war, there were two tea shops in Draethen, one owned by Mr and Mrs Billy Lewis, and the other by Mr and Mrs Billy Lloyd. These were used extensively by the soldiers from the castle, and when the Dutch troops arrived, they followed suit. Mrs Lloyd's garden was full of marigolds, and the first Dutch soldiers who visited the tea room thought it was in their honour, as orange was the royal colour (the house of Orange). The Germans had banned the use of the colour in Holland under their occupation. As each soldier left the tea-room, he picked a marigold and put it in his cap, looking very proud of the new badge. The following morning Mrs Lloyd's garden lay completely bare, but she didn't mind as long as it 'made the boys happy'. (Bernard Spooner)

When I was stationed in Holland towards the end of the war, I met a Dutch Sergeant Major, who told me that he had been at Ruperra. He spoke very highly of the hospitality his men had received locally. (Arthur Rogers)

In 1940 training begun for the Local Defence Volunteers (LDV), later re-named the Home Guard. Rifle drill, bayonet charging practice and drilling took place on the Tyn-y-Waun fields, often under the supervision of Bill "Pandy". Visits were made to Panteg Searchlight Battery for training in machine and Lewis guns, route marches and manoeuvres often being completed in the 6 o'clock field. Air raids were frequent in the summer of 1940, often during daytime when children were sent home from school to their shelters.

Aerial view of Ruperra Castle, at a time when the gardens were still cultivated. The castle had an open bakery where men were trained for duty in field bakeries abroad.

Mel Everson (Buzzer) was a member of the Home Guard and, during a training exercise in the 'W' wood, had to camouflage himself as a sniper up a tree. Evidently he did this well, but it was to no avail as his dog had found him and was sitting at the bottom of the tree, waiting for him to go home. (Bernard Spooner)

Mrs Billy Lloyd outside her tea room in Draethen.

The Bedwas, Machen and Trethomas Air Training Corps, to which many local lads belonged. Among the group here are Eric Bundy, Eldon Gadd, Roy Bodrell, Dennis Hartley, Hiram Everson, Derick Cross, Dennis Richards, Jack Gooding, Ernie Jones, Raymond Jones, Donald Harris, Douglas Everson, Jack Evans, B.A. Williams (Artie), Arthur Luke.

The ruins of the Waterloo Tin Works, 1952. Above the brick chimney stacks from the Tinhouse furnaces can be seen Waterloo Terace which was built in 1891 to house the tinplate workers. The tinplate with its brand name of Wynne was exported to many countries in Europe including Holland, Denmark, Norway and France.

The opening of the Rogerstone aluminium works in 1938, with its modern machinery, higher wages and regular working, attracted many Machen employees away from the Waterloo tin works, which closed in 1940. Exporting during war-time, together with lack of orders, and outdated machinery, all contributed to its decline. During the war, the works were used by the Admiralty for storage purposes, with a 'skeleton' staff staying on until 1950, when the remaining machinery was dismantled and dispatched, mainly to Pontypool.

During the war, the aluminium tin works at Rogerstone were considered to be a vital enemy target, and to offset the chances of bombing, oil burning fires were lit at points over quite a large area: Risca, Rogerstone and Pontymister. They would belch up terrific clouds of black smoke, and the smell and fumes were awful. When travelling home from Newport on leave, it was similar to travelling through dense fog. (Clive Coleman)

Just before the end of the war, Machen Women's Institute was formed, meeting in the early days at Machen house. In 1946, it moved to the old school house at Lower Machen, which was rented from the Tredegar estate. Rationing and clothing coupons remained for several years after the war, and activities included 'make do and mend'; this included renovating felt hats, making rag mats, string belts, sea-grass stools, wedge heel slippers, and cane work trays and baskets. By 1949, the WI had a hundred members, with more on a waiting list. In those post-war years, its practical approach was very popular. The purchase of a canning machine was a great event, and regular canning sessions were held in Lower Machen schoolroom.

Post-war – a new era

On 5 July 1948 a National Health Service became a reality, and the Monmouthshire County Chief Medical Officer, Dr Gwyn Rocyn Jones, who had visited Machen school many times in preceding years, commented it was difficult to understand the apparent lack of interest by many people in their own health. He said the first and greatest task to be overcome was to detect why large numbers of the population were immune to health education. Certainly that remark would not be made now!

At the beginning of 1949, a new sub-postmaster, Hubert Thomas, took over at Machen on the retirement of Mrs Edwards, daughter-in-law of Ebrill Edwards. The family had run the post office for sixty years from the same premises. The post office was now established at 'Le Vallon', 40 Commercial Road, once the home of Dr B.O. Barnard.

On the first day we received a telegram for a house in the Draethen, and Joan Soulsby (née Gray) who worked in the post office from the start, took a bus to Lower Machen, walked across the Traeth to Draethen, and delivered the telegram with exemplary promptness. On her walk back to the bus stop to Lower Machen, she was surprised to meet my mother on her way to deliver a second telegram for Draethen! As private telephones were such a rarity, the telegram service was essential for sending urgent messages. We also took over the responsibility for a 24-hour telephone service too. In 1949 the telephone numbers ranged from Machen 01 (Cwmnofydd farm) to Machen 50 (Machen quarry). (Doug Thomas)

W.H. Bishop's staff and lorries at Trethomas, with Bedwas Pit in the background, 1952. From left to right: Cyril Tuckwell, Keith Baynton, George Baynton, Maurice Hunt, John Hughes, Allan Williams, Dai Curtis, Lou Hibbs, Mr W.H. Bishop. This business provided an important and valued distribution service for vegetables and fruit. The latter was often used for canning, tinned fruit being rationed and very scarce.

Jim Everson (Jim the Post), delivering to Bill (Bee) and Noelene Stephens at Tyn-y-Waun Farm. Ralph Smith and Dick Bundy were later full time post-men, assisted by a number of part-time post-women. It was not unknown for the postmen to deliver mail on Machen mountain three times a day!

The opening of the village hall, 1949. Among the audience were Alf Wally, Cyril Williams, Judy Beeston, Jose Morgan, Bill Perrin, Mrs Perrin, Molly Worthington, -?-, Mrs.Jenkins, Tom Harding, Mrs Prince, -?-, Mrs Harold Beeston, Mrs Fred Brown, Gilbert Jones, Frank Shipley, Jack Morley, Ivy Morgan, Colin Prosser, Richard Williams, John Matthews, Reg Rees, Alan Elliott, Mrs Jenkins (Colliers Row), Mrs Edna Matthews, Mrs Mabel Wally, Mrs Shipley, Mrs Alma Harper, Mrs Lil Davies, Mrs Nancy Rees, Tom Rees, Ted Davies, Dai Davies, Vale Woosnam, Edmund Everson, Rita Williams, Beryl Wally, Arthur Jones (Laggin), Revd F.A. Oswell, Mrs Mary Oswell, Mrs Tudor Haywood, Mrs Talmage Edmunds, Mrs Annie Jones, Mrs Kate Thomas, Mrs Anita Beeston, Phyllis Davies, Mrs Miriam Davies and Mr P.O. Davies.

This was still the era of making one's own entertainment, and with the opening in 1949 of the Machen village hall, extra facilities became available for the Machen Glee Party, Women's Institute Choir, the Dramatic society and weekly film shows, in addition to church and chapel activities.

Siloam Baptist chapel had had serious disagreements with Revd Daniel Hughes back in 1936, and after that time struggled to keep going when, shortly before the war, he went to Detroit, staying there for some years.

My childhood memories were of the senior ladies who ran it, and I remember with a lot of affection, Mrs Harris, everybody called her Auntie Ede; Mrs Lil Rogers (Mrs Danny Rogers); Mr and Mrs Sydenham; Bert Sydenham; Mr and Mrs Bob Holland; and Mr and Mrs J. Jones (Snookie). Then followed Mrs Bissett and Linda Bissett and Muriel John. Whitsun treat on the Monday was always something to look forward to. Even in those days, the back part of Siloam was very primitive, so they used to go along ever so early to get the old big boiler stoked up for boiling water for dishes and tea. I remember the white china, it had a gold rim and a gold bow on it, and some for special days had Siloam stamped on it. The chapel itself, even when we were kids, was only opened on high days and holidays and for Whitsun anniversary.

During the 1940s, Mrs Holland did quite a few musical shows, and it really was a community thing. We also had a film and record club, run by Mr Sydenham, who was a coppersmith and did beautiful illuminated writing. He had a projector and we had all the old silents: Keystone Cops, Charlie Chaplin and Harold Lloyd. The records were usually highbrow, but we also had Spike Jones and the Laughing Policeman, we loved that. Siloam survived because of the efforts of all these people. Joe Jones used to take a service, and people would bring an interesting article from the Sunday Companion *for general discussion. (Liz Phillips)*

Presentation to Mrs Holland by the Revd Daniel Hughes, of a gold watch for long service as organist at Siloam Baptist Chapel, watched by Mr Bob Holland, Mrs J. Bissett and Mr Joe Jones.

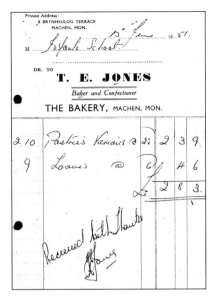

It was hoped in 1951 that the Festival of Britain, which was to be held in London on the south bank of the Thames, would boost morale and provide a cheerful break from the need to re-build homes, restore factories and provide jobs. Overshadowing this was concern for the health of George VI. He was unable to attend the celebrations in Wales, but the Queen (now the Queen Mother) came in his place.

Machen held a few events, which included a go-as-you-please fancy dress, a dance, and tea parties for pensioners and for children, and community hymn singing. The children were given a treat in the shape of a Punch and Judy show, provided by a Mr E. Bilson from Cardiff, for which the fee was £1 13s 6d. The price of foodstuffs and suppliers will bring back some memories.

Ted Brown supplied 25 pints of milk for 10s,
Emlyn Jones baked 144 varied pastries for £1 10s 0d,
Lloyd Harris provided 140 ice-creams for £1 12s 6d,
8 tongues and 13lbs of ham were supplied by W.G. Lewis of Bedwas for £4 17s 9d.

A few months after the Festival of Britain, on the 6 February 1952, George VI died at the age of 56. A new Elizabethan age was to begin, which was to differ greatly from what had gone before. The simple pleasures that many of us enjoyed would become commonplace, and almost forgotten, as life moved up to a faster pace.

One thing I remember about Good Friday, call it leisure or hard work, I don't know. We lived opposite Tom Llewellyn, the butcher, and Mr Cook, the baker, used to come down the night before, and at six in the morning, he would bring all the hot cross buns he had taken orders for. My job was to take these out in the basket, and I had one for myself. It was a great delight to have a hot cross bun, you looked forward to it, nowadays they are on sale all the year round. (Doug Hufton)

Dad always encouraged us to be good gardeners. We three boys all had our own patch of garden, which we dug and planted, and we were allowed to sell the produce for our own pocket money. I remember people coming to the house for new potatoes and we would go straight out and dig them up. The first peas, beans, blackcurrants for tart etc., was an event. Today it is taken for granted that they can be had most of the year. (Eric Coleman)

Whatever else may change in parish life, the village that still retains its school will always have a sense of continuity. Teachers and classes come and go, but school photographs have the power to re-kindle memories and friendships that have become faded with time. We hope the following selection from the 1930s and 40s will help you to do that.

School group, mid-1930s. From left to right, back row: Sadie Davies, Megan Morgan, Rita Williams, Hilda Morgan, Dorothy Davies, Anita Griffiths, Eluned 'Linned' Davies, Joan Watson. Third row: Ivy Green, Hilary Morgan, Dorothy Credgington, Dilys Morgan, Hilda Matthews, Gertie Williams, Anita Kellow, Beryl Price, Pattie Hill, Cynthia Williams, Terry Hill, Mr Spinks. Second row: Doris Bowen, Marie Rogers, Joyce Hill, Gwyneth Morgan, Peggy Bilton, Doreen Hucker, Lena Davies, Nancy Thomas, Joy Partridge. Front row: Dulcie Rees, Vi Attwell, Glenys Rowles, Gwyneth Dickenson, Mair Shapcott, Nora Goulding, Grace Lewis, Gaynor Davies.

1937-1938. From left to right, back row: Pamela Pope, Eirlys Rogers, Sybil Were, Mizpah Rosser, Marie Norman, Valerie Cave, Morgan Baynton, Heulwen Edmunds, Iris Gadd, Margaret John. Middle row: Barbara Morgan, Herbert Spring, Richard Williams, Clive Thomas, Bernard Spooner, John Jones (Graig), -?-, -?-, Fay Whittingham. Front row: Betty Perrott, David Woods, -?-, Byron Evans, Kenneth Davey, Royston Atwell, Tony Williams, Grosvenor Buckley.

From left to right, back row: Elwyn Edwards, Haydn Harris, Lloyd Jones, John Powell, Fred Rees, Tony Goulding, Graham Heath, ? Rudge, Miss Alma Gimblett. Middle row: Glyn Edwards, Roy Gooding, Anita Whittingham, Winnie Bowen, -?-, Henrietta Haskins, Violet Davies, Marjorie Greenhaf, Mavis Williams, Lyndon Jenkins. Front row: Ivor Morgan, Betty Burnett, Glenys Godel, Betty Thomas, Mavis Hall, Jean Morgan, Yvonne Sweetland, Iris Hughes.

Machen Infants, Class 2, 1947. From left to right, back row: Derrick Jones, Betty Burt, Raymar Everson, Robert Worthington, Robert Heath, Lynette Brown, Peter Davies, Cheryl Jones, Mary Stephens. Front row: Brian Richards, Kay Bowden, Rosalind Jones, Cheryl Baumer, June Davies, Derrick Dowdeswell, John Sweetland.

92

Machen School class, June 1942. From left to right, back row: June Deverrine, Mavis Hall, Myrtle Richards, Betty Burnett, Hilda Addis, Freda Watkins, Rosemary John, Pauline Sweetland, B.A. (Artie) Williams. Second row: May Keeler (evacuee), Eva Stephens, Jean Morgan, Lily Salmon (evacuee teacher), Violet Davies, Jean Morgan, Renee Perry, Lorna Noot, Molly Familoe. Third row: Lawrence Hawkins, Raymond Bowen, Clifford Baynton, Fred Rees, Grosvenor Buckley, Graham Heath, Roy Gooding, John Matthews, Roy Norman. Front row: Neville Lewis, Aneurin Rogers, Ken Rowles, John Colly (evacuee), Trevor Richards, John Jones, Gwyn Watson, Haydn Rees, John Rowlands.

Machen School class, 1945. From left to right, back row: Bayliss Davies, Kendrew Davies, John Maddocks, John Tamplin, Terry Shipley, Clive Bartholomew, Brian Griffiths, Billy Rowlands, Ron Shaw. Middle row: Barbara George, Margaret Williams, Emrys Podmore, Terry Alsop, Lawrence Norris, Graham Elliot, Douglas Street, Tommy Shaw, John Woodland. Front row: Juliet Rees, Vaile Woosnam, Mavis Jones, Edna Godel, Shirley Bayliss, Dorothy Richards, Margaret Williams, Freda Fullard, Margaret Spring, Moyna Evans.

Infant class, 1945-1946. From left to right, back row: Miss R. Perrin, H. Clarke, N. Griffiths, John Turner, Howard Bilton, -?-, Peter Williams, Roy Davies, Freddie Sweetland, Maldwyn Ellis. Middle row: -?-, Angela Whittingham, Rosemary Williams, Pamela Davies, Ann Rees, Joan Rees, JeanThomas, Julie Everson, Vilma Cole, Nancy Heath. Front row: Sybil Routledge, Yvonne Robbins, Joan Graves, Ann Green, Jenny Beacham, Pat Taylor, Joan Morgan, David Hill.

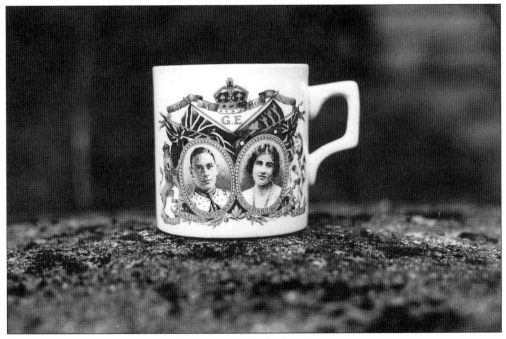

Coronation mug, depicting George VI and Queen Elizabeth, 1937.

Six

Modern Times

Many of the changes from the Machen of old to the Machen we know today originate from the early post-war period and the accession of Queen Elizabeth II. The first of these is the way television has invaded the life of everyone in the village and, as a consequence, affected the way we now live.

George VI's elder daughter, Elizabeth, our present Queen, was crowned on 2 June 1953. She had agreed to the televising of the whole day's celebrations, including the actual Coronation service, and for many in Machen it was a day to be remembered since the Wenvoe television transmitter had just been erected, enabling television sets to be installed for the event.

In common with others in the village, it was open house for the day. The television was in the 'middle room' and all available chairs had been crammed in there. I remember my father-in-law bought it from Herriman's in Caerphilly. The back door in those days was always open, unless weather prevented it or we had gone out. The kitchen table was in use all the time for sandwich making, and the kettle was boiled non-stop. Apart from the solemnity of it all, we were all so amazed to think that the cameras could show us so much. (Delphine Coleman)

The Queen and Prince Philip had visited South Wales a little earlier, on the 4 January, and drove through Machen on their way to Newport.

Alma Street and Napier Street Coronation Day party. From left to right: Mrs Muriel John, Mrs Morfydd Mullins, Mrs Peggy Edmunds, Mrs Doris Edwards, Mrs 'Flossie' Godel, Mrs Edie Graves.

The Railway

The 1950s saw the demise of the railway. Passenger services were the first to go, and eventually all the services to Brecon, Newport, Caerphilly and Pontypridd were closed. Machen closed to passengers at the end of 1962, and to goods in 1964, remaining in use for bulk freight until the Benzol plant, popularly known as the Bedwas plant, closed at Trethomas.

The only part of the railway line left now is the section from the quarry to the junction at Bassaleg, possibly the only standard gauge section of the old Brecon and Merthyr system of 1863 still in use.

There were a lot of protest meetings about the closing of the railway. People worked to the train times, they were so exact they didn't need watches. My father went to the meeting and said he worked by the train times, and someone said it would be cheaper to buy him a watch than pay compensation! (John Tamplin)

On one of my trips before the passenger line closed, I boarded the train at Trethomas. The carriage I travelled in was obviously of considerable age and upholstered in a red velvet type of material. The opposite seats of the compartment were so far apart that any passenger with fully stretched legs could not reach the legs of the person opposite. As the train approached Torpantau signal box, the train came to a halt. My compartment door was opened by the guard, who had walked down the line. 'Excuse me, sir,' he said, 'as you are the only passenger on the train would it inconvenience you if we stopped here for ten minutes?' I stated I was in no hurry, and the guard then explained that he had promised to cut a number of bundles of pea sticks for the signalman of the Torpantau signal box. The guard and the fireman went down the batter (bank) of the railway, and cut the pea sticks. Presumably the sticks were hazel, I think the month was April, just before the sticks were in full leaf. Meanwhile the driver had stayed with his locomotive. After a short while the train continued its journey, and as we approached the signal box, the whistle of the engine was blown and the pea sticks were thrown out. (Mr Glyndwr Jones)

Church Road signal box and yard at Lower Machen.

A sight never to be seen again: railway and road at White Hart, 1956.

The Quarry

This is still in operation as part of the Hanson group, and has extended greatly in area when compared to the early photographs showing just the one single face.

A distant view of the quarry. The site now extends to 123 acres and employs a work force of 175.

Crushing and screening plants are operated from a central control room with keyboard controls and closed circuit television.

New style trucks using part of the old railway line alongside Weavers Row.

Cray Valley Limited

In 1952 Coates Bros. opened what was locally known as 'the paint works'. Today Cray Valley Limited, is part of the worldwide Total Group, and a main provider of employment in the district. Site preparation commenced in 1948, and involved road widening.

It was wonderful; before that the road from Waterloo, after we got off the bus at the Round Tree, was so lonely. I used to be petrified, walking through the 'Bushy Park', there were trees, the raised road from the bridge to the arch, and the swamp either side. They had to re-build the bridge, and old Mr Caston from Chatham was night watchman. He used to hang lamps on either end. What a blessing – it gave light and you knew someone was going to be there, it was very scary before! Now it's more like Piccadilly Circus. (Liz Phillips)

The offices of the greatly extended Cray Valley plant today. The company is part of the worldwide Total-Fina-Elf group and is a valuable contributor to schemes which benefit the surrounding community. Its support to the Machen Remembered Society has been invaluable.

5 May 2000. Madison Shan of Machen School helps to bury a Millennium time capsule, containing items selected by the employees at Cray Valley, Machen and Rudry Primary Schools, Machen/Sautron Twinning, Bedwas and Trethomas Local History Group and Machen Remembered Society. It is planned that the capsule will be opened in the year 2050.

The Tredegar Estate

The final break up of the Tredegar estate, which had played such a vital part in the life of the village, commenced in 1951 when Tredegar house was sold, the rest of the estate being acquired by the Eagle Star Insurance Company in 1957. Many leasehold tenants were offered the chance to purchase their freeholds, and with the death of John, the sixth Baron Tredegar, in 1962, the connection with the Morgan family was ended.

The estate had provided work and homes for several centuries, and the Lords Tredegar had donated both land and money for the benefit of the whole community.

Tredegar gates were all perfectly hung in the old days. Two men would come all day to get it right for Lord Tredegar and his hunting. They had to swing shut without needing to be pushed. When the hunt went through they could be opened by the use of the stock (whip), without the riders needing to dismount. The letter 'T' was burnt into every gate. (John Tamplin)

In 1996 the Ruperra Conservation Trust was formed, to raise funds to purchase 150 acres of the old Tredegar estate, known as Coed Craig Ruperra. This ancient woodland commands magnificent views, and has been used both in Iron Age and Norman times as a defence point. In later times, the Morgans built a summer-house and garden walk on the site. Owing to the Trust's untiring efforts, the ground was purchased in 2000, and a proper management scheme for replanting this woodland has started. The walks to Ruperra, which were long gone, are now possible to Coed Craig Ruperra, which is open for all to enjoy.

A printed Christmas card, depicting Sir Charles Morgan and family inside Tredegar House, *c.* 1830. The house was sold in 1951 to the Sisters of St Joseph for use as a school, after being finally purchased by Newport Borough Council in 1974. It is now a fine social amenity for the area. (By courtesy of Tredegar House)

New Homes

The village had started to grow once again with the building of the council houses in 1927, and this continued after the war during the 1950s and 1960s, with the addition of Mountain View and Brynheilog; houses in Chatham and Llanarth Streets; Bron-rhiw; Graig View; houses, flats and bungalows in Fwrrm Road; the Graig-y-Rhacca estate; and finally, the bungalows in the Crescent in 1974. Glan-yr-Afon, being in the county of Glamorgan, was built in 1953 by the Cardiff authority.

Building the new estate at Graig View in 1955, with Judith Harris and Janet Sydenham making good use of the empty road for an extended playground.

The bungalows at Bron-rhiw built on the site of the Yard, which consisted of small cottages, at one time attached to the works at Machen Forge.

Shopping and the Family Car

Cars, lorries and an improving road network have taken over from the rail network as a means of distribution. This in turn has led to the growth of larger selling outlets, the super/hyper-markets. Some of these offer a free bus service which, coupled with the convenience of car ownership, has resulted in the disappearance of the many small shops which were part of the village scene. The small grocer, ironmonger/general store, ladies clothing/wool shop, and Co-op, have all had to bow to the inevitable. However, Machen still retains its 'Old Post' general store, a small grocery store and post office which are valuable assets to the community, providing local service and a friendly meeting place for many.

Above: The 'new' post office, with Mrs Lyn Greenhaf, in 2000. She took over in 1982 from Mr and Mrs A. Rogers, who had an ironmongery business there, prior to Mr Rogers being appointed sub-postmaster in 1971.

Right: The last small shop to close, was that of Ken Llewellyn, the village butcher, in the late 1980s. Apart from the high quality of his meat, the appearance of the shop at the end of the day took one back to another era, one of scrubbed counters, sparkling tiles and white paper hanging in perfect symmetry from the empty meat hooks.

Parish Life and Organisation

There were plenty of active organisations functioning in the 1950s and '60s, assisted as usual by the enthusiasm of certain dedicated people. The church had the Mothers' Union, Young Wives, Women's Hour, Altar Guild, a bell-ringers group, and a social committee. There was also an 'under-elevens club' and a First Machen cub pack, together with the Village Produce Association, Good Companions' Club, WI Dramatic society and St John Ambulance etc; the Workmen's club, the British Legion and the pubs too, all played their part.

Machen WI Choir in the early 1950s outside the Albert Hall. The group includes, from left to right: Mrs Wollon, Mrs P. Powell, Mrs Price, -?-, Anita Kellow, Mrs A. Harper, Dorothy Kellow, Mrs M. Bilton, -?-, Mrs E.M. Jones, Mrs N. Rees, Mrs Kellow, Mrs Edgar Rees, Mrs C. Jones, Mrs Fred Brown.

St John's Ambulance cadets, May 1953. From left to right, back row: Howard Bilton, Philip Sweetland, Dennis Rogers. Front row: Fred Sweetland, David Norris, Clive Williams.

When I joined the First Aid cadets (St John's Ambulance), in order to get money to buy our uniforms, a few of us used to go up to the ashtip at the Waterloo, taking my trolley which father had made. There we collected jam jars which were taken to our meeting place just behind the Co-op, and washed thoroughly. We were paid one old penny each. We also started collecting paper, again taking my trolley. We had a price from a firm who would come and collect when we had at least one ton. This took a lot of work and many journeys, so that it took us about nine months. We had to divide it into three separate piles: newspapers, magazines and cardboard; but to our dismay and disappointment, the reply from the firm was not what we had expected. The bottom had dropped out of the market, and they could not give us any money, although as a gesture of goodwill they would come and take it off our hands without charge! Still, we moved on and eventually had enough money to buy nearly every cadet a uniform. (David Norris)

The Revd F.A. Oswell retired in 1954 after a ministry of twenty years, during which time he had participated in many aspects of parish life. He was an excellent pianist and organist, producing many concerts and pantomimes.

He was a rector for the whole village. Although we were chapel-goers, he knew us by name, and when he saw our name in the papers for something we had done with chapel Sunday School, Guides or school, he would always stop and talk to us about it. My sister and I had terrific respect for him. (Liz Phillips)

Farewell presentation in 1954 to Revd F.A. Oswell. From left to right: Revd Oswell, Victor Matthews, Col. J.D. Griffiths, Mrs M. Oswell and Monica Oswell.

Gilbert and Sullivan

The Revd Oswell was succeeded by the Revd Fred Secombe, who had previously been curate in Machen from 1946-49. During his incumbency, considerable renovation took place at St Michael's and St John's, which was also re-decorated.

St John's was due to celebrate its centenary. Fortunately, in the village we had Mr Tom Bull, who had a high position in a building firm. He arranged for scaffolding to be put up to decorate the ceiling and organised bands of volunteers to remove the varnish from the pews ready for repainting. I remember having to be escorted down the ladders which were needed to reach the top of the platform in the roof, having succumbed to a large dose of vertigo! (Revd F. Secombe)

Rector Secombe also inaugurated the Machen Church Gilbert and Sullivan Society in 1956, which led to the church hall (church room still to many older folk) being altered. The room which had housed a billiard table was converted into a stage with excellent lighting equipment and backcloths by Tom Davies, Bill Panting, Cyrus Hughes and Peter Lathan, resulting in very professional and colourful shows. The repertoire also included *Die Fledermaus*, *Orpheus in the Underworld* and *La Belle Helene*.

What a hectic life we are leading just at present. We spend Saturday after Saturday working to the noise of hammers, electric drills, saws, sewing machines and the welcome rattle of tea-cups, while a hard-working team of men and women struggle to finish the big stage renovation job that was begun just after Christmas. In addition to all this, costume making is in full swing, trying on this, measuring that, amid wails of 'I don't measure all that, I'm sure' and 'I can't have put on three inches since last year'.' (Mrs A.L. Oxford, parish magazine, 1965)

The Gondoliers, with Gondolier Fred Secombe and Joan Case. From left to right: Rosemary Lovell, Glenys Godel, Vi Harper, Bert Johnson, Betty Harris, Edith Haywood, Alice (Topsy) Oxford and Eddie Williams.

Sport

Machen Rugby Club and Machen Cricket Club have both celebrated their centenaries. The rugby club continued to use the old reading room for all its activities until 1997/98, when a new pavilion was built adjacent to the bowling green. This was a joint venture which won Lottery funding, and provided changing and catering facilities for the rugby, cricket and bowls clubs.

Machen Rugby Club, 1952/53. From left to right, back row: Jack Davies, Roy Burnett, Ernie Jones, Harold Harris, Trevor Burnett, Ron Gooding, Bob Whittaker, Noel Filer, PC Tom Price, Ralph Durston, Terry Lewis, Ramsey Carter, John Shapcott, Chris Harris, Hector Thomas, Des Lowe (trainer), Arthur Davies, (chairman). Middle row: John Hicks, John Pink, Jack Gooding, Graham Jones (captain), Ken Lovelock, Roy Bodrell, Bev Whittingham. Front row: John Edmunds (Tal), Jimmy Bedford, Lloyd Jones, Roy Gooding, John Fletcher, Roy Harris, 'Ottie' Williams.

Machen Rugby club, 1955/56. From left to right, back row: Tom Allsop, Jack Kibby, Bryn Hicks, 'Silent' Ron Jones, John Shapcott. Second row: Jack Davies, Harold Harris, Terry Alsop, 'Teg' Harris, John Hicks, Peter Davey, Bev Whittingham, John Edmunds, Arthur Davies, Mr Richards (referee), David Alsop. Third row: Ray Rosser, Jimmy Kyall, Lloyd Jones (captain), Ken Rogers, B. England. Front row: Tony Hughes, Brian Were, Lloyd Worthington, Malcolm Earley.

The old jest that 'Machen Rugby Club changes in one county and plays in another' is, therefore, no longer the case. The reading room is now the 'club', a meeting place for members, and the past players who mainly make up the committee have seen that it is extremely well maintained.

The cricket club continued to play their games at Lower Machen, but a new pitch laid in the recreation ground adjacent to the new pavilion, with an all-weather wicket and double bay net, has brought cricket into the centre of the village. At the present time, the cricket club, with the help of Sports Chest, has six newly-qualified coaches running a junior section of under 11s, 13s and 15s, with sixty members from Machen and the surrounding area, which augurs well for the future.

Machen Cricket Club, mid-1950s. From left to right, back row: -?-, Alf Sayzeland, Dilwyn Evans, John Hicks, -?-, Tal Buckley (umpire). Front row: Ken Snell, Ken Harrington, Reg Henley, Dennis Spargo, Don Harris, Terry (TD) Everson.

Machen Bowling Club. From left to right, back row: John Gough, Peter Goddard, Bernard Mardell, Rees Holmes, Roy Williams, Roger Watkins, Tom Pugh, Gordon Carter, Peter Cooksley, Pat Jones, Malcolm Wakeley, R. Tidridge, Mal Williams, Owen Williams, P.Williams, Gordon Thornton, George Turnbull. Front row: Donna Gough, Marian Goddard, Marian Williams, Sheila Mardel, Myra Price, Ann Gunning, Clarice Carter, Sue Thornton, Jackie Cooksley, Etta Murray, Jean Jenkins. The Club was formed in 1985, and five years of intensive fund-raising led to the bowling green being opened officially in June 1992.

Education

Due to the changes which have taken place at secondary, technical, college and university levels, Machen children of secondary age now attend Bedwas Comprehensive, which opened in 1962, Maesycwmmer (Bedwellty) being given a new catchment area. Bassaleg Grammar School and the adjacent Graig Secondary Modern School, which opened in 1958, amalgamated in 1970, and the whole campus is now known as Bassaleg Comprehensive School.

Machen junior school has continued to be a focal part of the community, absorbing curriculum changes that encompass the use of television and computers. Teaching of the Welsh language is compulsory, and there is now a nursery class, and a school uniform has been introduced.

Local history is one of the school's many strengths, and the Machen Remembered group has been glad to help by sponsoring a competition and providing information whenever it is needed. The school holds its own Eisteddfod every year, and all the children participate in drama, poetry, writing and singing classes which culminate in chairing the bard. The playground, once just an ordinary patch of tarmac, has been transformed by painting of imaginative and constructive games for infants, together with provision of bikes and scooters. Machen's railway heritage is acknowledged in attractive murals on the walls, and a gardening club is one of the most recent and popular activities which has resulted from the enthusiasm shown in the construction of a Millennium garden.

Machen School class, Standard 1, 1955. From left to right, back row: Maurice Rogers, Richard Burt, Beverley Oram, Reginald Young, -?-, Michael Harris, Bill Jenkins, Jeff Price, John Banfield, Alan Rogers, Stuart Rogers, Keith John. Middle row: Eva Roberts, Kaye Roderick, Sandra Berni, Jackie Dowdeswell, Lesley Mogridge, Marilyn Jones, Elizabeth Edmunds, -?-, -?-. Front row: Anthea Williams, Elaine Jenkins, Jeanette Moses, Eileen Rogers, Gabriella Motta, Jayne Green, -?-, Ann Thomas, Betty Davies, Margarette Maggs, June Baumer.

School class, May 1957. From left to right, back row: Derek Jones, Desmond Beacham, Laurence Jones, Jeffrey Bull, Courtney Fox, Jeffrey Matthews, Melvyn Young, Jeffrey Price, George Hughes, Stewart Dickinson, Howard Davies, Mrs Eileen Stuart Jones. Second row: Ken Allsop, Roy Williams, Margaret Llewellyn, Carol Greenhaf, Julie Pocock, Allison Reynolds, Jackie Mogridge, Jennifer Hawkins, Janet Greenhaf, Graham Jones, Dorian Moyle. Third row: Gillian Jones, Carolyn Moore, Susan Jones, Christine Fallaize, Christine Phipps, Linda Whittington, Jean Harris, Glynis Jenkins, Sandra Dickinson, Denise Shapcott, Linda Evans, Joan Burt. Front row: Clive Johns, Gareth Beacham, John Matthews, Graham Bolton, Gordon Bolton, Adrian Blakeborough, Dennis Copeman.

Machen School winners of Road Safety Competition, with Mr H. Moses, Clerk to the Bedwas, Machen and Trethomas Community Council, Mr E.F. Pearce, Chairman, Mr C.J. Phipps, Councillor, Michelle Reed and Owen Williams, 1984. (*South Wales Argus*)

School football team, 1995/96. From left to right, back row: Christopher Riley, James Roden, Bradly Young, Amy Lawrence, Ross Cooper, Adam Davies, Richard Everson. Front row: Richard Jones, Barne Povey, Anthony Parsons, Tavinder Kakavada, Daryl Hopkins, Dale Frantzeskou, Matthew Hall, Steven Everson, Michael Wallace.

Girls' cross-country group. From left to right, back row: Samantha Morgan, Sofia Anthanasiou, Victoria Maher, Sian Williams, Claire Riley, Rebecca Nash, Madison Shan. Front row: Amee Davies, Sara Edwards, Ellen Burnett.

110

Machen had to overcome and adapt to the loss of old faithful works, services, shops and chapels. In 1974, the old Bedwas and Machen UDC, which had pioneered so many worthy projects for its inhabitants, disappeared, only to be absorbed into the Rhymney Valley District Council under a new Local Government Act. This put Machen into Mid-Glamorgan, although the postal address became Machen, Gwent. This situation was to last until 1996 when, once again, there was change and the village became part of the new Caerphilly County Borough Council.

During this latter period, in 1989, there was an attempt to 'reclaim' a disused colliery spoil heap on the Risca side of Machen mountain. The Machen Mountain Action Committee campaigned vigorously and successfully against this on the grounds that the ancient pillow mounds and platform houses were at risk, together with the Ridgeway walk.

There has also been further building adjacent to New Row (Tudor Gardens), but by far the largest development has been the new Riverglade estate, built on the site of Tyn-y-Waun, which had been a market garden for some years. The development consists of 126 homes of varying size and design, and necessitated the building of a bridge to connect with the main road. This was an undertaking that required widening the river near the Fwrrwm Ishta with much heightening and banking work. It was a source of great interest to the many who watched its construction.

View of Machen Mountain, and the area in dispute, showing the 'tips'.

The new bridge being placed in position.

In keeping with the modern trend, few of the houses on the Riverglade Estate have chimneys, as central heating is now a way of life.

My husband (Albert Lovey Vines) worked at Bedwas, first at Britannia at Pengam. Pits have gone, good thing really, although you miss the coal fire. There was one young man years ago, I think he was selling something, and I said, 'Come on, just step inside,' and he saw I had a coal fire. He came up the steps, and I said 'Come in and have a warm if you like'. He said 'It's the first time I've ever seen a coal fire'. He was thrilled to bits. I asked him to sit by it. I know I shouldn't have done it, but in those days we never thought bad of anybody, did we? I can see him now, he 'coopied' down, you know, there's a Welsh word for you. He was ever so pleased. (Mrs D. Vines)

This touching reminiscence by one of Machen's old residents, sadly no longer with us, mentions several of the changes that have come over village life today.

During the last twenty-five years or so, the village has moved from being a close-knit community to a wider and more fragmented one. The statistics gained from the 1991 census showed that forty-one percent of us work outside the district. This inevitably leads to the oft-repeated phrase 'I don't know half the people in the village any more', which is the pattern in many places. Mobility gives access to leisure facilities which are professionally presented on a grand scale, but the existing village organisations still keeping going, and any event organised for a worthwhile charity will find Machen folk digging deep into their pockets.

Whatever the future holds for Machen, this journey through the past will, we hope, have been a pleasurable and thought-provoking one. What a heritage it has, and what characters it has produced, who have carried their skills to many parts of the British Isles and to the world, when leaving its confines.

A stranger approaching Machen, whether it be from far away or from 'up the valleys', might think it was a village typical of South Wales, a little more scenic than some perhaps, within its setting of woods and mountains, but we know better, don't we? We cannot really understand or appreciate what is around us, if we have not discovered the secrets of what has gone before.

Then and Now

The workshops adjacent to Machen Station with: ? Price, Stan Thomas, Harry Gadd, Jesse Curtis, Matt Curtis (?).

Above left: John Coleman, Harry Gadd and Jack Davies by the Brecon and Merthyr North end sidings, with Machen foundry siding to right in the photograph.
Above right: The footpath to the old Vedw step-bridge, dismantled in the early 1990s.

Machen Girl Guides, 1954-1955. From left to right, back row: Pam Davies, Caroline Brown, Elizabeth Williams, Diana Mullins, Mrs Mary Brown, Gillian Askey, Mrs Olive Beeston (captain), Heather Brown, Ann Rees, Jean Thomas, Joan Graves. Middle row: Raymer Everson, Barbara Beech, Sheila Edwards, Ann Bavin, Ann White, Nancy Heath. Front Row, Sheila Beeston, Jean White, Vera Harris, Barbara Kingdon.

April 2000. Machen brownies seen here outside the old village hall before renovation. From left to right, back row: Fay Hewitt (young leader), Doreen Howells (guider), Helen Watkins (guider). Middle row: Katie Owen, Bethan Pugh, Sian Jones, Kirsty Rogers, Melanie Riley, Ceri Williams. Front row: Sarah Kirton, Danielle Davies, Hannah Powell, Sian Williams, Tayah Clarke, Asha Kidley, Victoria Maher, Chloe England, Sofia Anthansiou, Laura Sigsworth, Sara Jones, Vanessa Turner.

The whole of the John family, seen here at Park Farm in the 1920s, on the occasion of Lewis John's emigration to New Zealand. From left to right, back row: Elias, Thomas, Mary, Lewis, Jack and Henry. Front row: Elizabeth, Celia, Mrs Mary John, Mr William Henry John, Margaret and Hannah.

Group at Top Corner, New Row, in the 1920s, with the communal bake-house on the right. From left to right, back row: Mrs Tuckwell, -?-, Mrs Humphries, Mrs Elizabeth Richards, Mary Jane Jones, Granny Davies, Mrs Partridge, Mrs Meredith, 'Lou' Humphries, Mary Ann 'Tootsy' Humphries, Lottie Davies. Front row: -?-, Fred Davies (?), -?-, C. Harris.

Carnival float at Green Row, early in the twentieth century.

Festival of Britain float in Commercial Road, 1951.

116

A Rare Trio

Above left: Mrs Agnes Spargo and Dick Hyndman outside Dranllwyn Cottage. This is the only photograph found showing the old cottages with their sash windows and chimneys which were pulled down to build Lsywen. The Hyndmans worked in Machen forge during the mid-nineteenth century, living there and at Cae Bach.

Above right: An old iron hoop and guider which, no doubt, travelled up and down many lanes and pathways, like the Dranllwyn, spurred on by its youthful owner.

Left: Mr Herbert Sweetland, seen here in the yard of Russell Stores during the 1940s, was kept busy in the days when kitchen ranges were the norm. He charged 3s to sweep one chimney, but 2s 6d if there were more than one.

Flower show, 1960s. From left to right: Graham Beeston, George Cooper, Esau Davies, Tom Voyce, -?-.

Machen Floral Group at their first year's show in 1985. From left to right, back row: Joyce Davies, Jan Smith, Joyce Williams, Dorothy Davies, Jean Owen, Liz Phillips. Front row: Gill Hooper, Doris Rees, Brenda Maslin, June Clayton, Flo Gowland, Betty Knight. This popular group has now disbanded, and donated their remaining funds to provide new curtains for the church hall.

118

The Maypole dancers in the carnival procession to celebrate the Silver Jubilee of King George V in 1935.

A ticket for the Jubilee Dance.

A well-known group of Machen stalwarts: Alderman E.B. James, Tom Harding and Idris King, enjoying a British Legion fête.

Two founder members of the Machen Remembered Society: Lloyd Davies and Arthur Rogers. Lloyd recorded faithfully, over the years, village life in film; while Arthur recorded his memories on paper for his children. This gave the initial impetus to start up Machen Remembered. Arthur was also a valued treasurer for several years.

Lower Machen, winners of the Tidy Village competition, late 1960s. The group includes from left to right: Joan Jenkins, Percy Jenkins, D.L. Jones, Robin Herbert (unveiling the plaque), R. Treasure, Col. K. Treasure, Mrs E. Price, Miss M. Jones, Mrs S. John, W.H. John, Mrs M. Pritchard, Miss O. Beeston, Anthony Anstey, Sandra Anstey, Graham Beeston, Caroline Jenkins, Mrs J. John, Mrs B. Anstey.

Lower Machen post office in the late 1940s, with Elizabeth (Lizzie) Edwards, Mrs H. Beeston (post mistress), and Jane (Jinny) Edwards, who delivered post in Draethen and Lower Machen for many years. Also seen here, is the local head postmaster.

Machen and Sautron Twinning ceremony at Sautron, France, 1993. From left to right, back row: David Billington, John Chilcott, Eileen Chilcott, Dawn Whitehead, Marilyn Hobbs, Colin Hobbs, Pam Coccihara, Keith Morgan. Front row: Heather Morgan, Liz Phillips, David Phillips, Annwen Chilcott, Chairman of Rhymney Valley District Council.

Members of Probus, 1995-1996. From left to right, back row: Roger King, Richard Bond, Hugh Lougher, David Morgans, Charles Lintonbon, Bill Read, Ron Wathan, Bert Iles. Fourth row: Tom Pugh, Byron Jones, Ray White, Bernard Mardell, Merlin Jones, Frank Birch, Goff Clayton, John Gibbons. Third row: Lyn Short, Arthur Coleman, Dennis Platt, Peter Fincher, Rex Major, Ron Osborne. Second row: Lloyd Davies, Granville Pitman, A. Rogers, Lloyd Jones, David Phillips, Victor Willis, Bernard Smith. Front row: Ron Walters, Ken Hooper, Matt Morrissey, Gordon Westcott, Tom Grocutt, Geoff Edmunds.

The Mothers' Union with the Revd Clifford Warren and Mrs Sylvia Warren, taken shortly before Revd Warren's retirement. He served Machen faithfully as Rector from 1976-1997, and introduced the ever-popular Christingle service, while Mrs Warren ran a successful Sunday School throughout his ministry. From left to right, back row: Revd and Mrs Warren, Audrey Adams, Ida Lane, Eileen Pugh, Rhona Stacey, Donna Gough, Shirley Warbrick, Flo Gowland, Joy Jenkins, Mair Thomas, Carrie Matthews. Front row: Rita Pugh, Betty Phillips, Dorothy Jones, Denise Wright, Ithwen Heath, Ceridwen Myers, Vi Rogers, Dolly Vines.

The new incumbent's board at Lower Machen was dedicated on 29 September 2000, by the Dean of Monmouth, the Very Revd Dr Richard Fenwick. From left to right: Revd F. Secombe, Revd Denise Wright, Dr R. Fenwick, Revd P. Morgan, Revd A. Silverthorn, Revd Canon P. Vann, Rector of Machen, E. Nurton, Hon. Verger.

Opening of the new Machen surgery in 1997. From left to right: Dr A. Napier, Jane Billington, (practice manager), Drs I. Morris, D. Bailey, D. Lewis and W. Chaudhry.

The Rugby Club committee, 2001. From left to right, standing: R.K. Davies (chairman), P. Rees (club captain), A. Roach, S. Moore, A. Lewis, R. Williams, G. Rosser. Seated: P. Williams, D. Perrott, M. Workman, R. Blenkiron (secretary).

View of the new village hall and library, built with an impressive grant from the National Lottery, together with committee and council funding. The hall has extra space for meetings and classes geared for all ages, while the much-increased library area offers computers with internet access, in addition to books, videos etc.

The former Chairman of Caerphilly County Borough Council, Cllr Mary Hughes, alongside Mrs Lillie Whittingham, Secretary of Machen Community Centre, opening the new village hall and library on 23 March 2001.

Epilogue

I remember, I remember,
The house where I was born...

Do you remember, did you know...?

...going to the Roman well below Rhydgwern farm for fresh watercress

...the skilful way fruit tarts were made. Sugar was added after the pastry was cooked, the knack was to slip off the top put the sugar in, and flip the top on without breaking the crust

...the population of Machen rose from 1,371 in 1841 to 2,997 in 1891

...one old penny would buy a pomegranate, complete with a pin to get the fruit out. If you only had a halfpenny, you were given half a fruit and no pin

...in the days when you had farthings, especially in the haberdashery shops, you were given a card with pins on it, rather than a farthing change

...how women cradled the loaf against their chest when cutting, rather than using a bread board

...the use of paper for spills, and also wound into a tight plait to start the fire

...how potent rhubarb wine could be, particularly that sold at the Maypole. The number of bikes still stood outside in the early hours testified to the inability of their owners to ride home!

...throwing up sticks to knock the conkers down from our beloved local landmark, oblivious to the traffic passing by you on the Forge road

...getting frog-spawn from the Vedw pond, or the Pickle pond (sometimes known as the Piddle pond), and the old leat pond near the Pandy

...how very little wood was ever left lying around on roads or paths, it was always gathered up for kindling, or morning wood, for kitchen ranges

...there were people in the village who could charm warts away. No magic appeared to be performed on the person with the wart, but burying a piece of meat in the garden certainly did the trick

...Joe, the ice cream man who came around on a motorbike and sidecar which converted into a serving area for the ice cream, and Mitch who had a hand cart

...that coal drams coming from the old pit in Green Row passed so close to the Four Houses, (Woodbine Terrace), that you could put your hand out of the window and touch them

...potato picking, often in the rain, with an old hessian sack over one's head and shoulders to keep out the damp

...visiting the coal tips to pick up coal and sticks (broken pit props), dodging the coal and stones after the buckets released their loads, then loading up sacks and using toboggans to drag the coal back home

...black-leading the grates, lifting up the coconut matting with all the dust falling through to the floor, before taking it outside to shake

...being able to go out and leave your doors and windows open

...that oral tradition has it that the conker tree was planted between 1820 and 1840, by a William Thomas of Draethen, a woodman working for the Tredegar estate, who also planted much of the large 'W' woodlands near Rhydygwern. The number of rings would appear to closely correlate to this date. Could it have been planted for the Coronation of Queen Victoria?

Coronation mug, Queen Elizabeth II, 1953.

Sources

Newport Reference Library (*South Wales Argus* and other local papers, trade directories, census returns, maps etc.); the National Library of Wales, Aberystwyth; the Tredegar Estate records; and the County Records Office, Cwmbran. Also, parish records, including registers, poor law accounts etc.; county education minute books; the tithe map; Machen School log books; and the diaries of W. Beechey and P.T. Woodruff.

G. Beeston, *Bedwas and Machen, Past and Present*.
Glyndwr G. Jones, *Cronicl Caerffili*.
Raymond Howell, *A History of Gwent*.

Acknowledgements

We acknowledge with gratitude the help we have received in the preparation of this book from all those who generously recounted their wonderful reminiscences. We are deeply indebted to Messrs Lloyd Davies and Glyndwr Jones, who have donated photographic material from their records, and to Bernard Smith, who has spent many hours photographing, preparing slides and developing film for us. We also thank Mr S. Phillips, who willingly offered photographs from his railway collections, together with Mostyn Bennet and Tom Grocutt for artwork and geological information.

Tribute should also be made to the late Mrs Alice Edmunds, without whose reminiscences this book would be much the poorer, and to the late Mr Graham Beeston who persuaded her to record them fifty years ago.

The names of all those who kindly allowed their photographs to be used are as follows:
Mrs I. Baumer, Mr K. Baynton, Mr R. Beach, Miss M. Beeston, Mr R. Bodrell, Mr C. Bowen, Mr R. Burton, Mrs C. Carter, Mrs B. Clark, Mrs D. Cook, Cray Valley, Mrs D. Davies, Mrs I. Denty, Mrs E. Dickinson, Mr B. Evans, Mr and Mrs H. Fallaize, Miss I. Gadd, Mrs G. Godell, Mr D. Griffiths, Hanson Group, Mr D. Harris, Mr J. Hicks, Mr T. Hughes, Miss L. Hunter, Mr A. Jones, Dr A.E. Jukes, Mrs M. Jeremiah, Mr H. Jones, Miss M. Jones, Mr R. John, Mr P. King, Mr K. Llewellyn, Mrs A. Foight-Lloyd, Mrs J. Lorimer, Mrs R. Lovell, Mrs C. Matthews, Mr H. Morgan, Mrs M. Morse, Mrs E. Murray, Mr D. Norris, Mrs B. Onions, Mrs B. Palmer. Mrs K. Panting, Mrs F. Partridge, Mr E. Pearce, Mrs B. Phillips, Mrs Liz Phillips, Mrs J. Picher, Mrs A. Price, Mrs R. Pugh, Mr A. Rogers, Mrs E. Rogers, Mr J. Rowlands, Mrs L. Rymer, Mrs B. Shilleto, Mr A. Spargo, Mr and Mrs H. Spring, Mr L. Short, Mr J. Sweetland, Mr C. Tamplin, Mr D. Thomas, Revd Canon P. Vann, Mrs M. Walter, Mr G. Westcott, Mrs N. White, Mrs J. Wintle, and Mrs D. Whitehead.

We wish to record the ongoing assistance given to us by Mrs Mary Tiffin and the staff of the Bedwas Centre, and Mr Martin Jones on behalf of Cray Valley.

Our sincere apologies if anyone has inadvertently been omitted.